RESHAPING RETAIL

For more information about this book please visit
http://reshaping-retail-book.mckinsey.com

RESHAPING RETAIL

**WHY TECHNOLOGY IS TRANSFORMING
THE INDUSTRY AND HOW TO WIN
IN THE NEW CONSUMER DRIVEN WORLD**

STEFAN NIEMEIER,
ANDREA ZOCCHI,
and
MARCO CATENA

WILEY

Cover design: Andrew Ward
© 2013 John Wiley and Sons Ltd

Registered office
John Wiley and Sons Ltd, The Atrium, Southern Gate, Chichester, West Sussex, PO19 8SQ,
United Kingdom

For details of our global editorial offices, for customer services and for information about
how to apply for permission to reuse the copyright material in this book please see our
website at www.wiley.com.

Wiley publishes in a variety of print and electronic formats and by print-on-demand.
Some material included with standard print versions of this book may not be included in
e-books or in print-on-demand. If this book refers to media such as a CD or DVD that is
not included in the version you purchased, you may download this material at http://
booksupport.wiley.com. For more information about Wiley products, visit www.wiley.com.

Designations used by companies to distinguish their products are often claimed as
trademarks. All brand names and product names used in this book and on its cover
are trade names, service marks, trademark or registered trademarks of their respective
owners. The publisher and the book are not associated with any product or vendor
mentioned in this book. None of the companies referenced within the book have endorsed
the book.

Limit of Liability/Disclaimer of Warranty: While the publisher and author have used
their best efforts in preparing this book, they make no representations or warranties with
respect to the accuracy or completeness of the contents of this book and specifically
disclaim any implied warranties of merchantability or fitness for a particular purpose. It
is sold on the understanding that the publisher is not engaged in rendering professional
services and neither the publisher nor the author shall be liable for damages arising
herefrom. If professional advice or other expert assistance is required, the services of a
competent professional should be sought.

Library of Congress Cataloging-in-Publication Data is available
A catalogue record for this book is available from the British Library.

ISBN 978-1-118-65666-2 (hbk)   ISBN 978-1-118-69882-2 (ebk)
ISBN 978-1-118-69883-9 (ebk)   ISBN 978-1-118-69888-4 (ebk)

Set in 10/14.5 pt Palatino by Toppan Best-set Premedia Limited
Printed in Great Britain by TJ International Ltd, Padstow, Cornwall, UK

CONTENTS

FOREWORD

Mobile Internet access is growing at 20 percent annually. Seventy-five percent of all shoppers research purchase-related information online. The world's top five social networks have a combined total of 2.5 billion members, and millions are joining their ranks every day. Why should retailers care about these trends?

Because they put powerful technology in the hands of shoppers—to compare prices, place orders, and post reviews—anywhere and anytime. In effect, the power balance between those who sell and those who buy is shifting. Even seasoned retail executives are in awe of the fundamental nature of this change. Their questions go to the very core of the retail industry: What is the future role of the physical store? Which of today's retail formats will survive? What will set the winners apart from the losers? How can retailers benefit from evolving technology and changing shopper behavior? In short: How, if at all, can retailers survive the technological revolution we are witnessing?

In this book, five of our most distinguished retail experts from around the world consolidate McKinsey's perspective on those pressing questions. James Naylor of London, Stefan Niemeier of Hamburg, Roger Roberts of Palo Alto and Marco Catena and Andrea Zocchi, both of Milan, have joined forces to compile our latest thinking regarding, for example, constant connectivity, the next big data frontier, cloud computing, channel convergence, and the emergence of an "internet of things." To challenge and expand their own observations and conclusions, the authors have also invited leading practitioners to provide their perspectives on how technology is changing the face of the industry, from big box retail and online pure play to content aggregation and search.

In 2011, *Retail Marketing and Branding: A Definitive Guide to Maximizing ROI*, now in its second edition, launched our book series *Perspectives on Consumer Industries and Retail* to great acclaim. It is my privilege to present the second book in the series, *Reshaping Retail*. Like the best of its kind, this book is rooted in a profound understanding of technological trends, but it truly stands out by examining their impact from the perspective of the CEO. I hope you share my excitement about this compendium—and will be encouraged to seek out future volumes in the series.

Klaus Behrenbeck
Director, McKinsey & Company, Inc.
Leader of the European Consumer Sector

Introduction

The modern retail system has worked to dazzling effect. From the 19th century, store owners emerged from small beginnings to set in train an industry that has seen some operators become nationally, even globally, dominant. Along the way, they turned retailing into an art, and then a science. Their development was assisted by the lowering of tariff borders and the multiplication many times over of international trade in consumer goods. Efficiency gains enabled by improved production techniques, communications, and information technology reinforced a virtuous cycle of lower real costs and thus prices. Now retailers in emerging markets appear to be repeating the story all over again, except on a scale and at a speed beyond anything we have seen before.

Given all of this, it is hard for those of us who work in retailing to accept that the industry as we know it is living on borrowed time, on the brink of transformation. But that is the view that prompted us to write this book, a view that has been sharpened and reinforced as we researched it. We have spoken to many of our clients and colleagues who are engaged directly in this intense period of transition. What they told us further confirmed both the urgency with which conventional store-based retailers must now act and the extent of the challenges this change represents in strategic, organizational, and above all technological terms. For the industry is in the grip of a revolution powered by digital technology. This will be as big in its effects as the mercantile revolution that saw the birth of retailing as we know it, and the Industrial Revolution that kicked off the modern era.

Retailers' operations have long been underpinned by technology—telecommunications, bar codes, electronic data interchange—so why the commotion now? From our perspective, there are two reasons for it. First, technological innovation hitherto has served primarily to help retailers do what they have always done, but better. They have become ever more powerful intermediaries between suppliers and customers, able to operate at ever-greater scales. Paradoxically, today's technology threatens that power and hence the entire business model. Second, many traditional, store-based retailers still do not understand today's technologies, let alone tomorrow's—they are retailers, not technology companies—and so are unprepared for the speed of change that is about to hit. That is why the subject merits a book that puts the developments into context and describes the driving forces behind them, the nature of the change, and what store-based retailers must do to transform their strategies and operations to thrive.

To begin the book, we pull the camera back a long way, showing how deep are the historical roots of today's business model. Since the Middle Ages, retailers have relied on what is largely a push system of stock movements. The retailer, be it a merchant with a horse or the operator of a nationwide supermarket chain, anticipated future demand, selected the goods to meet it, and then organized delivery in a place where people would buy—first the marketplace, then dedicated stores. Technology did not interfere with this process. It just made the process more efficient.

To understand why this is changing, it is, we believe, important to grasp the underlying technological drivers of change at a reasonable level of detail and to learn how a particular combination of separate innovations has been so powerful. So we describe the ways in which advances in computing power, storage capacity, and network connectivity are driving three preeminent, parallel, and mutually reinforcing trends that will define the digital era of retailing. The first, mobility, will be powered by the availability of technology everywhere: in stores, at home, on the go. The second, measurability, will see far more activities in the value chain, not least consumers' behavior, being measured more accurately.

And the third, agility, will come from the development of cloud computing, which enables companies to develop systems (often the roadblock that slows progress in improving business processes or pioneering new business models) with speed and ease.

The technology generating these trends will help retailers improve their processes and contrive new experiences for consumers to a degree previously unimaginable. But it is also ushering in new competitors and empowering customers. And it is customers who are the focus of much of this book, for retailers of every hue will have to contend with the power that now lies in customers' hands. Individuals can browse, select, pay, and take possession, all without entering a store. But this is only a small aspect of what has changed. Far more significantly, new technologies have put an end to the information asymmetry between retailers and consumers. In short, customers have been empowered at the expense of swaths of retailers.

It is not all bad news—far from it. Consumers will still want to visit certain stores for many of the same reasons they already do: convenience, sociability, and even the ability to buy cheap goods (yes, we believe that some store operators will be able to match online rivals on some goods in a digital world). And the measurability that technology delivers will make information productivity as important as capital and labor productivity have been to the industry, helping to drive retailers' efficiency and their ability to serve their customers well to new heights. But at the center of the business model will be the customer. This is not customer care. It is customer-centricity. Absolutely everything in the operating system—pricing, promotions, assortment—will be touched by customers' needs recorded in real time, requiring a degree of responsiveness most commercial directors would find impossible today. In some respects, customer-centricity means returning to the kind of thinking that prevailed when owners of small stores bought the merchandise they knew individual customers would like. Retailers sacrificed this intimacy in favor of scale, as technology emerged to help them manage more complex operations more efficiently. Now they have to manage both.

This will place extraordinary pressure on retailers, because all sorts of skills and practices and ways of making decisions, in some ways unchanged for a century or more, are fast becoming redundant or are only partly sufficient for profitable success. Perhaps toughest of all for many of today's store-based operators will be the technology requirements. Organization-wide fluency in and with technology will be a critical success factor for retailers everywhere, and the robustness and flexibility of their IT systems and the transparency and ease of use of their digital interfaces will be as important as the aspects of physical retailing that are familiar to us today: location, store format, size and layout, point-of-sale design and capacity, in-store promotions, and more.

Ultimately, success will hinge on more than competence; it will come down to a way of thinking. Customer-centricity will need to be valued not just by the store owner, as in the past, but also by all employees in the organization. It will need to become embedded in their daily tasks. The same applies to technology, which must be at the center of the organization and recognized as such by everyone. As one senior executive of a global online retailer told us, "If I were forced to choose, I'd say we were a technology company rather than a retailer." Store retailers will, in essence, need to change their DNA. We hope this book helps them understand why—and inspires them to make the transformation now.

Chapter 1

A Brief History of Retailing

Co-authored with James Naylor

Today's senior retailers have endured a series of profound shocks and changes. During their careers, they have witnessed the dot-com bubble of the late 1990s, been swept along by a credit-fueled consumer boom, felt the pressure of financial markets' expectations of cross-border retailing, and been blasted by the macroeconomic consequences of a capital market crash and its aftermath. Those who struggle for economic survival day by day and week by week may feel they have had enough history already. Nevertheless, although these words may be of little comfort, the events have been merely the birth pains of a new era in retailing in which the retail landscape will change completely.

To understand this assertion, it helps to consider the nature of today's changes in the context of the history of retailing. We can organize our thinking by dividing the time line of retailing into three eras: the mercantile, the modern, and the digital. The era of medieval mercantilism was born of an embryonic banking system that made capital funding available for the first time and steadily increased the scale and scope of trade over centuries. The modern era, from the Industrial Revolution to the turn of the 21st century, ushered in mass production and the consumer society. In the present era, which got under way 15 or so years ago, another revolution is taking place: the conventional ways of retailing laid down and consolidated over the course of centuries are being thrown over in favor of a new order founded on three technological pillars—computing power, networking, and data storage capacity. We refer to this as retailing's digital era.

Retailers are by definition intermediaries, helping suppliers to find a market for their goods and customers to buy what they need or desire. In the mercantile and modern periods, retailers' role as the intermediaries between suppliers and customers—adding value to both and extracting profit for themselves in the process—was necessarily a narrow one. Retailers served a small, elite class of people until, progressively, more members of society moved beyond subsistence to become consumers. With the help of capital, new management techniques, and new technology, they grew steadily more skilled in that role, and steadily more powerful. The more skilled they became, and the greater the demand, the greater the scale at which many were able to operate while still delivering on the most fundamental requirement of a successful retailer: to match the flow of goods with information about supply and demand in order to earn the highest possible return on the money invested in inventory.[1] This was as much the challenge for the merchants of the Middle Ages who bought wool in England and sold it in markets in Bruges or Ghent as it is for today's retailers who operate hypermarkets of up to 220,000 square feet.

But in the digital era, the retailer's role as intermediary is under threat. Fifteen years ago, the new technologies that promised so much for e-commerce did not quite deliver, and the dot-com bubble burst. Today, a mature range of digital technologies is sending the industry a clearer signal. And these technologies are game changing. Traditional retailers no longer hold the monopoly on marrying information about supply and demand with the appropriate flow of goods. That truth is already apparent in the declining importance of the bricks-and-mortar store, which once embodied the convergence of the two. A new army of online retailers now harnesses the power of computing and the Internet both to aggregate demand online and to fulfill it. Understanding how retailers' power as intermediaries grew through the course of history helps explain why today's technology is so disruptive and brings home the magnitude of the changes afoot.

The mercantile era

The traveling merchant of the late Middle Ages was the first recognizable retailer in the sense we understand the term. For centuries, his predecessors in trade had taken products they had made to markets and fairs, by foot or horse or ox, and sold them directly to local people. In contrast, the retailer who emerged in Europe in the 13th century was a middleman, buying goods from producers and selling them from town to town and village to village. For most people, however, many if not all of their material needs were provided through self-sufficiency. In a largely urban, post-industrial society, we readily forget a world of smallholdings and subsistence, in which informal barter was as important a means of exchange as money transactions.

Under the most basic model of business in this era, the merchant financed his own operations and carried out his own freighting activities. He bought goods from specialist centers of production (such as linen from Reims), organized mule trains to traverse mountain and plain, and distributed his wares through markets, fairs, and networks of peddlers. The expansion in money supply as silver production in Europe increased in the 13th century enabled him to go farther and expand his business. Venture capital had arrived, increasing the scale and scope of trade and bringing about the first wave of internationalization.

Eventually, sea routes pioneered by the great voyages of discovery in the 15th and 16th centuries enabled this merchant's successors to reach around the globe, exchanging an ever-widening variety of goods. By the beginning of the 18th century, Europeans had become accustomed to fabrics from India, tea and porcelain from China, lacquer work from Japan, and tobacco from America, as well as more locally produced imports, such as wine from France. Of course, these were luxury goods, or at any rate staples only for the very rich.

At the same time, these retailers were gradually being relieved of the need to spend long periods away from home, thanks to resident merchants, who began acting as agents for purchase in sourcing markets such as Bruges, Genoa, and Casablanca. And the emergence of dedicated providers of transport freed merchants to concentrate on selling their goods. Two types of generalist businesses took root: mercers, who provided haberdashery items such as silks and linens, and grocers, who supplied dry food provisions, household goods, and hardware. There were dealers and the precursors of what we would call shops, but for several centuries, there was little separation between wholesalers and retailers. Business was carried out in proximity to both domestic living areas and workshops for craft production. Gradually, particular towns and even streets became associated with specific commodities: London's Haymarket was home to traders of hay and straw, for example.

The founding of the great international trading enterprises, following the great voyages of discovery, brought a surge of imports into Europe and a progressively stricter delineation between wholesale and retail. The East India Company, established in 1600, cleared its stock with regular auctions, consciously rejecting the opportunity to develop a full "retail" activity. That opportunity was available for others to take.

Hence, by the 18th century, shops had become a common feature of London and Paris. In London, certain streets, notably Cheapside, were becoming dedicated to retail, while in Paris, covered shopping arcades, or *passages*, were established. The shop owners understood what goods were available and selected those that would meet customers' needs or that customers might like, because much was new to the market. And because each merchant knew most customers by name, it was relatively easy to purchase stock that was likely to sell. There was little that resembled mass production, even by the middle of the 18th century.

Craft manufacture remained entwined with merchandising and selling: a shop would have a workshop behind or above it, and products tended to be made to order and customized. But the merchant-retailers who owned a general store in the village or town spread their sourcing footprint wide in order to link producers as well as other merchants with consumers. The accounting records for one such store—Abraham Dent's shop in Kirkby Stephen, a small town in Yorkshire, England—show just how extensive sourcing networks were. During the period covered by the accounts, 1756 to 1777, Dent stocked a range of dried grocery items (tea, sugar, flour), as well as wine, brandy, soap, candles, and a limited range of textiles.[2] He could loosely be said to have commissioned his own "private label" for stockings. What is most striking is that Dent drew his stock from 175 suppliers in 48 towns and cities across England. The mercantile era had advanced a long way.

The modern era

The onset of the Industrial Revolution in the mid-18th century marked the beginning of a long wave of change and technological innovation, from the telegraph to the computer, which endured until the turn of the present century. It saw the development of retailing from Abraham Dent's provincial general store to the hypermarket chain bent on overseas expansion and the vertical retailing model of the Spanish clothing brand Zara as globalization shrank the world at the close of the 20th century. Each development in between—the department store, the mail-order catalog, the self-service supermarket, the edge-of-town category killer—represented an advance in consolidating the power of the retailer as mediator between supplier and consumer. Only the retailer could match supply and demand on a large scale and thus sell at low prices, profitably.

Consumer society

At the start of the Industrial Revolution, conditions were ripe for the creation of a more consumer-oriented society. As in the mercantile era, mediation between manufacturers and customers defined the retailer's role. What changed, and would continue to change, was the scale of its operations.

The period marked rapid advances in manufacturing efficiency as industrialization harnessed human capital and automation to replace the craft economy with mass production. Goods began to be produced in larger quantities. In addition, items that hitherto had been expensively imported luxuries could be readily copied. Chinese porcelain is the obvious example. For years, Chinese producers alone possessed the manufacturing knowledge to combine kaolin, feldspar, and quartz at very high temperatures. But a combination of research by German chemists and the observations of a French Jesuit who traveled through China led to the first European production of porcelain, in Meissen, Saxony. Other centers of production quickly became established. In the southwest of England, china manufacturing emerged in Bristol, using kaolin (or "China clay") from Cornwall. More famously, Josiah Wedgwood set up production in Stoke-on-Trent. Comparable advances were made in the manufacture of textiles, furniture, and ornaments. As economic historians have pointed out, this "imitation" of Asian technology was a distinctly 18th-century virtue for Europeans—the equivalent of what we would now call "teardown."[3]

The Industrial Revolution saw a social revolution, too, characterized by the emergence of a new proletariat and of the cities in which they lived. The slow growth of a consuming class accelerated until this demographic eventually outnumbered and surpassed in economic significance the traditional agricultural laboring classes. A tier of administrators, clerks, and other functionaries emerged in parallel—all ready to consume affordable versions of luxury items. The same course of events is now unfolding in the world's emerging markets, although at an extraordinary speed in comparison.

Transformed communications, including transportation systems to carry messages, also underpinned the rise of consumerism. The underlying transportation technology did not change (it was still the horse), but better roads and transport scheduling made a vast difference to the ways in which economic agents could communicate with one another. Thus, a journey from London to Manchester took some three days in 1750 but just 18 hours by 1836.[4] When the railways arrived, the effect was even more striking. Markets opened for perishable commodities, for example; so back in Manchester, the greater supply of fresh fish from the coast caused the price of fish to fall by 70 to 80 percent.[5] Information flowed faster, too. With retailers better informed about what suppliers had to offer and what customers might want, they could arrange to have the right goods delivered more quickly.

The emergence of specialist retailers

The rise in both supply and demand created conditions for the emergence of more specialist retailers, choosing to sell a certain range of goods in order to build distinctive value propositions. But this innovation required some important enabling steps in the new urban centers for retail, which emerged first in London and then in cities across Europe and North America: municipal investments in paving and lighting, as well as the gradual realization by city authorities and private developers alike that the construction of specialist shopping areas served their economic interests.

The department store

The most prominent subtype of specialist retailer, the department store, arose from the activities of textile retailers as they extended their range and enlarged their shops in the early and middle years of the 19th century. It was a dramatic development, and contemporaries were well aware that something new was emerging; they often described these businesses as "monster shops" or "monster houses."[6] But the specific identity of the department store developed from a concept of universality that went beyond a broad range of clothing categories.

The first generally recognized department store in this sense was Bon Marché in Paris. It was a single-site operation—but on an unprecedented scale—that moved into progressively larger premises. By the 1870s, when it was located on the city's rue de Sèvres, it had become the world's biggest retail business by sales, the primus inter pares (first among equals) of monster shops.[7] The store showcased the cutting-edge practices of its day by adhering to fixed prices (reinforcing its position as a trusted intermediary) and placing advertisements in newspapers to spread the word about the vast array of goods for sale. In turn, advertising, particularly from specialist retailers, enabled newspapers to expand rapidly.

Around the world, retailers copied the department store format. In London, William Whiteley, who started out in 1863 with a single drapery store, followed the monster store route by acquiring adjacent shops to offer a total of 17 different departments. In Chicago, Marshall Field's opened in 1887. Another Bon Marché was established in Seattle in 1890, and Harrods, which had blossomed from small beginnings in the first half of the nineteenth century, progressively rebuilt in London's Knightsbridge in 1905 to arrive at the store we know today.

The department store was one of society's most influential institutions and a beacon of modernity. Initially, it was characterized by volume as well as breadth of range, and the aggregation of a large number of items enabled department stores to offer low prices. Besides leading change in the availability and assortment of goods, department stores were early adopters of numerous new technologies; in America, they were among the first to use mechanical data-processing equipment to analyze sales. They also pioneered methods in areas such as inventory control, credit policy, promotional techniques, and hiring practices. In addition, the department store showed how, by aggregating sufficient demand, it could make increasingly efficient use of the capital invested in stock and construction.

Bon Marché customers were affluent, middle-class people who in no way represented the newly industrialized masses. A different format arose to serve the larger numbers of urban workers on lower incomes. Frank Winfield Woolworth started out as a stock boy in a general store in Watertown, New York, in which one of the most successful elements was a table on which every item was priced at five cents. When he ventured out on his own, in Utica, New York, in 1879, he established an entire store based on that single-price premise. The business initially prospered but was unable to withstand a hike in rent. So the next year, in partnership with his brother, he opened a store in Scranton, Pennsylvania with a sign outside reading, "5¢ and 10¢ Woolworth Brothers Store." It was the first nickel-and-dime store.[8] Whereas the department store was the first format subtype to be copied internationally, F. W. Woolworth in 1909 became the first modern retailer to export a retailing concept, opening a shop in Liverpool in the northwest of England.[9]

The mail-order catalog

In America, the wide distribution of population created the conditions for the development of the first modern catalog retailing operation: Sears, Roebuck & Co. built a comprehensive remote operation from focused origins in watches and jewelry. The business, founded in 1893, anticipated much of the context in which Internet retailing would emerge more than a century later. It featured a distributed network of customers, a central inventory of goods of a wider range than would be practical—or economical—to stock across a diffuse network of stores, and a reliance upon delivery and what we would now call return logistics. Sears and other catalog businesses showed that, by using centralized stockholding, they were often better able to match stock levels to demand than were traditional stores.

The self-service supermarket

Perhaps more significant than the development of the department store was the foundation of the supermarket and the concept of self-service, which would revolutionize food distribution globally. A notable example is Piggly Wiggly, a business in the southern United States that opened its doors in Memphis in 1916. By introducing the first self-service model, allowing customers to assemble their orders themselves, Piggly Wiggly enabled its managers to focus on refinements such as the best use of display space, price levels, and the types and frequency of promotions.

Although Piggly Wiggly is credited with being the first self-service grocery store, it was not quite a supermarket—that implies greater scale and, in turn, more customers, and customers buying more. There are a number of candidates for "first supermarket." Terry Sharrer, a historian from the Smithsonian, bestows the honor on a business called King Kullen, based in Queens, New York, which had the appealing tagline "World's greatest price wrecker."[10] As far as we can see, there are some strong rival candidates. The Hattem's store in Los Angeles began life in 1927 with many of the features we still associate with the format, including staying open 24 hours a day.

King Kullen's boast serves as another reminder of how scale has historically worked in retail. Really low prices attract disproportionate numbers of customers. The retailer is able to cope with the volume because it operates in stores of sufficient size and with sufficient choice to meet their requirements, while being able to sell at those low prices because of scale economies. Scale also gives retailers more information about demand—in the case of supermarkets, that flow of information is almost constant—which helps them turn stock faster. These retailers match flows rather than individual parcels of investment in inventory in their attempts to balance supply and demand, helping them to meet the all-important metric of gross margin return on inventory.

Over time, the central role of fresh foods in supermarkets required regional—and then national—operators to become increasingly sophisticated in the management of integrated chill-chain distribution. In addition, as logistics abilities developed, there was a move to centralize distribution and consolidate goods in retailer-owned distribution centers, rather than have them delivered directly from suppliers to stores. The short life of fresh foods and the importance of optimizing the use of space proved compelling drivers of change: for much of the past century, most of the technological and information-processing innovation in retail has emerged from the supermarket sector.

The edge-of-town category killer

Category killers took scale in a different direction, focusing on a much narrower range of goods to push prices lower still. Car ownership was the factor that made the emergence of this format possible, for the category killer was the monster store of suburbia. Situated on the edge of or outside cities and large towns, US companies such as Toys "R" Us, Best Buy, and Home Depot laid claim to preeminence in one retail category after another. Modern retail software systems that help control stock and monitor sales performance have enabled these businesses to maintain an efficient operating model. But category killers also illustrate some of the limitations of operating at very high scale with a relatively narrow range of goods. Prices in these stores are so competitive and margins so thin that the companies are vulnerable to relatively small falls in demand. In consumer electronics retailing, the shift in purchasing from store-based retailers to digital retailers has already had a dramatic effect on the retail landscape.

The hypermarket

The biggest format of all was the hypermarket, or its US cousin, the supercenter. Just as the supermarket was the expanded version of the self-service Piggly Wiggly, so the hypermarket is the supermarket writ large. If a supermarket represents 20,000 to 30,000 square feet of space (and this varies from market to market, as a US supermarket can be at least 50 percent bigger), then a hypermarket can range over areas from 50,000 to 220,000 square feet. The most telling difference, however, is not size per se but the prominence that hypermarkets give to nonfood goods. If this category's sales account for 10 to 15 percent of a supermarket's turnover, that is not a bad performance, but in a hypermarket, nonfood items can represent as much as 25 to 30 percent.

When did the hypermarket first emerge? Conventional histories tell us that Carrefour opened the first true hypermarket in the Paris suburb of Sainte-Geneviève-des-Bois in 1963.[11] Carrefour was strongly influenced by local competitors that were also operating supermarkets with nonfood items. But the French retailers learned much from a charismatic figure, the Colombian Bernardo Trujillo, a retail guru at the cash register manufacturer NCR, who ran courses for retailers from many countries to train them in the new science of "modern merchandising marketing."

It is remarkable how many of the overseas visitors to Trujillo's conferences in Dayton, Ohio were from France, and his effect on French retailing was striking. Within the context of selling more cash registers—NCR's principal purpose—he offered modern retail management prescriptions that were a kind of codified set of lessons gleaned from US supermarkets. It is partly due to him that French retail distribution, which was on a significantly smaller scale than that of the United States in the early 1960s, leapfrogged US practices. Only in 1988 did Wal-Mart, which had developed a huge discount store business based on nonfood items, finally add a full range of fresh foods to create the supercenter.

This was the format that quickly gave Wal-Mart dominance in the US national grocery market, combining the systems used in supermarkets and category killers to sell a dazzling array of goods at rock-bottom prices at scale. Centralized logistics are the key. The flow of goods is streamlined so that working capital is used more efficiently, while accurate sales forecasting enables restocking to respond to demand so that, as far as possible, items arrive just in time. The company demonstrated what could be achieved through the mastery of the coordination of information and material flows.

Vertical retail

In various retail sectors, but most notably perhaps in clothing, more and more retailers have pushed into the sourcing and production of a range of goods made exclusively for them, the better to coordinate the two. Likewise, some manufacturers have taken control of their own distribution in their own retail stores. Somewhat confusingly, the industry uses the term *vertical retail* to describe both activities.

Italian manufacturer Benetton may have been the pioneer of this approach in clothing. However, the best-known and most frequently cited exemplar is Spain's Inditex, which has an operating model first developed for the company's Zara brand, which opened its first store in A Coruña, Spain in 1975. Zara's end-to-end retail business model arguably takes the coordination of information to a new zenith: the company famously describes itself as "selling in production," meaning it can reorder lines that are especially popular and have them delivered to stores within days. Since rolling out its first overseas outlet in Oporto, Portugal in December 1988, Zara has become a truly international brand with, at the time of writing, 1,659 outlets in 84 countries. On its website, Inditex says, "The retailer's international footprint proves that national borders are no hindrance to a shared fashion culture." Globalization did not prove so easy for all retailers in their pursuit of ever-greater scale, however.

Globalization

The retail industry has been a global one for centuries, with retailers amassing goods from around the world to delight their customers. But in the middle of the 1990s, capital markets developed tremendous expectations for cross-border expansion by leading retailers that had saturated their markets at home. Investors wanted to see mergers and acquisitions or rapid organic growth abroad.

The managers of leading retailers, many of whom had no experience in the markets concerned, found themselves under pressure to make major strategic decisions while at the same time managing significantly increased complexity. As they attempted to do so, the markets drew conclusions rather abruptly. Thus, Tesco, although it later proved to be an adroit and enterprising global retailer, had its growth prospects marked down for a number of years because of one relatively unsuccessful attempt to expand into France.

Contrary to investors' initial expectations, the value that had been attributed to overseas expansion proved generally hard to substantiate. One reason was the elusive nature of scale economies in cross-border retailing. Despite the apparent logic that greater volumes of goods should command lower unit prices from manufacturers, the relatively low value of most everyday purchases and the high costs to transport the goods meant that such aggregation existed more in theory than in practice. There is no value to capture in trucking something that can be more cheaply manufactured locally.

It also turned out that certain tastes and consumption habits are remarkably resistant to change, especially those concerning food and food preparation. This spelled trouble for grocers, who happened to be the very largest retailers—the ones upon which the greatest hopes for cross-border growth initially were pinned. In contrast, retailers that sell newer types of products, especially within consumer electronics, have been able to educate generations of new customers globally. What unites us across the world in using a smartphone or tablet computer is not something we share in preparing our evening meals.

Following these hard lessons, the almost frantic intensity of hopes resting on cross-border expansion for the largest traditional retailers has lessened, and the markets have become more discerning. Quietly, and with a few steps backward in addition to the ones taken forward, a good number of leading retailers have continued to expand their international businesses ever since. In fact, while many had believed that internationalization required huge scale and the replication of formats, experience finally taught them that what really matters is local scale and formats more closely aligned with domestic consumer needs.

The digital era

Although foreign landscapes continued to tantalize many, retailers next turned their attention to the online environment, and straightaway many believed the digital revolution would prove as transformative for retailing as its industrial predecessor had been. The term *new economy* quickly permeated thinking and generated an investment boom in another pioneering form of retailing, e-commerce. Even the most basic of the initial propositions for digital retail caused tremendous excitement among entrepreneurs and investors, with both groups sensing the arrival of something very significant. This enthusiasm for all things e-tail explains how, on the day of Webvan's IPO, its shares closed at a price that implied the company was worth $8.45 billion.[12]

The excitement stemmed from the fact that retailers and consumers could now exchange all the information required for making a decision to purchase and carrying out the purchase transaction without the customer being present at the premises of the retailer, while catalogs had started to dematerialize. But during the early years of e-commerce, the infrastructure, consumers, and retailers were not ready to operate in this context at scale. As a consequence, the boom became a bubble, which burst.

On first studying business, many students learn of the great speculative bubbles of the past, some of which sound inherently ridiculous. How could the Dutch have been so naive as to drive a speculative boom in tulips during the 17th century? How, in the early 18th century, could so many Britons have lost fortunes in the South Sea Bubble, or Frenchmen let themselves be fooled by the Mississippi Bubble? But with the passing of time, and upon reflection, we can concede that in each case there was real wealth to be made in the markets concerned. Some 350 years after the tulip boom, the Dutch continue to have the largest spring bulb industry in the world. Likewise, the global trade envisaged by the South Sea Bubble did come to pass, and belief in the economic potential of America has been fully vindicated.

So, in the aftermath of the dot-com bubble and the resultant technology crash, many incumbent retailers, including some that had been painfully slow to embrace the new consumer technology, have started to build meaningful businesses online. And what is surely clear to all is that the digital revolution is transforming the role of the traditional retailer. Demand is no longer aggregated only in the physical store, but online too. Meanwhile, the likes of Amazon, by offering such a huge, undefined range of products, have ridden roughshod over the idea that a key role of every retailer is to make a careful selection of the products that its particular customers want or might be enticed to purchase.

E-commerce has not been the only concern of retailers in the digital age. As early hopes for the Internet dream began to fade and management attended to the requirements of international expansion and category and service diversification, many retailers looked to internal efficiency and differentiation to sharpen their value proposition. Tesco, for example, became more aggressive on price and customer benefits while trimming costs. This resulted in significant revenue growth, market share gains, and increased profitability. In some countries, and with the help of technology, retailers evolved by streamlining operations and opening new stores that operated more efficiently than their old ones. In doing so, they helped improve the overall productivity of an entire market, as Wal-Mart did in the United States.[13]

The financial crisis of 2008, with the resulting economic downturn, not to mention the associated negative consumer sentiment, has been traumatic for retailers. After all, to make the majority of their sales in developed markets (and an increasing proportion of those in developing markets), retailers depend upon consumers' willingness to make discretionary purchases, not just their ability to pay for necessities such as food. The shift toward shopping for value has been marked, customer loyalty has weakened, and volumes have contracted.

Despite the importance of these economic constraints, we believe that the most powerful trends demanding the attention of the retail industry's leaders will involve what is happening with technology. Indeed, so strong are the forces at play here that we believe the 2001 crash was merely a question of timing. Future historians will dismiss it as a blip as they describe how the digital revolution caused a third upheaval in retailing. And while the mercantile and industrial eras strengthened the position of the traditional retailer, the current upheaval may turn out to have a very different impact. The technology that has taken large retailers to new levels of power and centralization (often at the expense of small, independent retailers) is now, in its latest iteration, beginning to leech power from them.

We may marvel at the optimism of the first generation of e-commerce start-ups that tacitly assumed old brand loyalties could be displaced overnight. Many were indeed exceptionally careless with capital; few really understood the means by which retailers actually create value. But they were right to think something had changed. What was it?

Notes

1. Retailers know this as the gross margin return on inventory (GMROI), the return on average working capital investment in inventory. It explains why fast rotation of low-margin inventory is, at least arithmetically, equivalent to slower rotation of higher-margin inventory.
2. T. S. Willan, *Eighteenth Century Shopkeeper: Abraham Dent of Kirkby Stephen* (Manchester: Manchester University Press, 1970).
3. For example, M. Berg, "From imitation to invention: Creating commodities in eighteenth-century Britain," *Economic History Review* 55, no. 1 (2002), pp. 1–30.
4. Roy Porter, *London: A Social History* (Cambridge, MA: Harvard University Press, 1998).
5. D. Alexander, *Retailing in England in the Industrial Revolution* (London: Athlone Press, 1970), p. 17.
6. The terms were especially used by smaller traders. Here is *Freeman's Journal and Daily Commercial Advertiser* for September 23, 1851, approvingly quoting a piece in the *News of the World*: "A great [and] wide-spreading evil . . . in almost every provincial town . . . of immense shops, founded by men possessing large capital, who seek to conduct under the same roof the sale of various articles. These monster houses are absorbing all the business formerly carried on in the smaller shops."
7. It still trades on the same site.
8. For non-North American readers, Americans call 5-cent coins nickels, and 10-cent coins dimes.
9. His expansion was rather like building one's first overseas hypermarket next to the airport, for Liverpool was the first mainland port of call for transatlantic shipping.

10. Dr. Terry Sharrer used a five-factor definition as the test of what constitutes a modern supermarket: self-service, multiple separate departments, cash and carry, discount pricing, and multiple stores. Terry Sharrer, personal communication, 2012.

11. The name Carrefour comes from the French word for roundabout, because the first store was named for the project site, and it took its name from the roundabout it overlooked.

12. Troy Wolverton, "Webvan delivers on the Street," *CNET News*, November 5, 1999, http://news.cnet.com/2100–1040–232534.html.

13. As Brad Johnson noted in his 2002 *McKinsey Quarterly* article, Wal-Mart in 1987 "had a market share of just 9 percent but was 40 percent more productive than its competitors as measured by real sales per employee," in Brad Johnson, "The Wal-Mart effect," *McKinsey Quarterly* (February 2002), pp. 40–41. A series of Wal-Mart innovations in electronic data interchange and supply chain practices would be copied by competitors in the industry, but Wal-Mart's growth alone changed the productivity of the retail sector in the United States.

Chapter 2

Technology: The Crucial Retail Enabler

Co-authored with Nina Gillmann

B efore turning to the technology-driven changes that lie ahead, it is worth contemplating what technology has already delivered and, importantly, the manner in which it has created value for retailers. This exercise will help distinguish the technology which has long under-pinned the prevailing retail business model from the technology which is transforming it.

Technology has long played a pivotal role in retailing. While the retail innovations of the 19th century may seem remote now, the period's early department stores were beacons of modernity and often the first busi-nesses to make systematic use of the latest technologies. They were the Apple flagship stores of their age.

In Paris, the expansion in 1874 of the site on boulevard Haussmann of the first Printemps store saw the introduction of elevators.[1] The store was one of the first to use electricity for illumination, and—significantly for a design that so enthusiastically celebrated modernity—customers were able to view the store's very own power plant from behind a glass wall. Two decades later, the store was able to boast a direct connection to the Métro.

The mastery of innovations such as lighting, cooling, escalation, and elevation was essential for the running of large, modern stores, releasing retailers from the constrained spaces at the front of the ground floors of terraced high street buildings. The stores blossomed into cathedrals of commerce. But as imposing as Printemps and its fellow *grands magasins* undoubtedly were, their operations pale by comparison with the advances made by huge retail chains over the past 50 years, principally the radical scaling up in the manageable size of stores enabled by information technology.

"Information" is the key word. Successive waves of technology have put more information at retailers' disposal, allowing them to do more efficiently what they have always done. In essence, technology has helped them to be better intermediaries, able to better manage the physical flow of goods because of better information about supply and demand. This added transparency is what has enabled retailers to operate efficiently at such scale. The very concept of the modern retail chain involves the sequencing and coordination of massive physical and information flows across extended networks—impossible without the data transfer, storage, and analytic capacity afforded by modern computing power, telecommunications, and integrated software.[2]

How retailers add value

The extent to which this is true becomes more apparent when the retail business model is examined in detail. Retailers add value as intermediaries in four ways: by preselecting goods for sale, by aggregating demand, by offering sales advice, and by physically moving stock to the point of sale. These activities represent the defensible territory of retailers—the means by which they have been able to make money. This territory is what technology previously reinforced and is now subverting.

Preselection

Preselection is the set of decisions that, in sum, represents the retailer's "editorial signature." In any given product range, the retailer presents customers with a variety of goods, often introducing customers to products they previously would not have thought to buy. This offers several advantages to suppliers. First, their goods are marketed in an appropriate context, meaning they will be broadly relevant to customers who come to the store in search of specific items—and may even complement or be substituted for the customers' original choice. In addition, the retailer provides sales staff to explain the product and answer questions. If the retailer is trusted by consumers, the supplier's goods are endorsed by the retailer's reputation, too.

Some retailers maintain a relatively slow-moving assortment of items, while others make goods available one day and remove them the next. Some cover multiple categories of goods, and others specialize in just one. But in simple terms, there are two types of activity: editorial direction and editorial choice. Direction involves the decision to stock a certain type of product or to sell items that have a given range of prices. Choice entails a finer discrimination between close alternatives.[3]

Retailers' knowledge of their customers creates value for both customers and suppliers in these selection tasks, as their insight into customer behavior, derived from their own observations and their possession of transaction data, helps them to improve greatly the match between supply and demand. The fact that so many retailers have learned to sell their data to their suppliers indicates the data's worth. Some go further, providing data to market research agencies, which then provides syndicated data to data providers, as well as abbreviated versions to third parties, such as consultants.

Demand aggregation

The ability to gather enough end-users or consumers at a single or several points of sale is known as demand aggregation. As a result of it, suppliers enjoy access to more consumers, in more markets, at a lower cost, and they have a good gauge of how much to produce. This in turn can make them willing to sell their goods for less. For consumers, retailers' bargaining power with suppliers enables lower prices than any consumer would be able to negotiate alone.

We tend to think of scale in terms of many hundreds, or even thousands, of stores, but the ability to make a consistent offer, sometimes over very large areas, is mainly an individual-store-level phenomenon, and each location must be capable of attracting sufficient demand to justify its particular collection of items for sale. Retailers tend to think of scale solely at the level of retail chains, and thus of many hundreds or even thousands of stores. But just as individual customers can visit only one branch at a time, so the ability to make a consistent and compelling offer of goods for sale and related services is always expressed in terms of single stores. The retailer must assure the perfect execution (assortment, price, and sales support) at store level in order to attract enough customers into each store. Each must offer enough to prospective customers to justify their investment of time, and attract enough of them to make its own existence viable after meeting the costs of rent, salaries, local taxes, and other store-specific costs, as well as covering the cost of the items sold and the cost of bringing them to the back door of that store. Only then, after establishing a successful format and offer, can the retailer scale up successfully.

Of course, the traditional retail business model accomplishes demand aggregation by anticipating future demand and buying for it in advance. However, it is almost impossible for retailers to order just the right quantities at the right times. Consequently the price of demand aggregation has been the carrying cost of merchandise to assure availability of products to consumers and of markdown to clear slow-moving items.

Sales advice

Traditionally, the most cost-effective and convenient location for providing sales advice, be it explaining how to use a gadget or which product to choose, has been at the point of sale. From the shopper's perspective, retailers' stores have been, more or less, comfortable, accessible, and safe environments in which to consider purchases at leisure and seek advice. In contrast, while manufacturers may have far more knowledge about their own products than the retailer, they generally know less about selling to consumers and, critically, cannot easily coordinate with competitors to agree on an appropriate range of goods from which the consumer may choose. The merchandising context is sometimes as helpful to the customer as an explanation or advertising claim. After all, if we can see what good, better, and best actually look like with examples, we have a better understanding of the choice we are being offered. All of this gives the retailer a significant opportunity to add value.

Physical movement of stock

The fast and efficient delivery of stock through complex networks that can include warehouses, stores, and home delivery and return collection services can drive down transportation and inventory costs and, ultimately, end-user prices. In the past, stock movement was often the shared responsibility of manufacturers, logistics specialists, and retailers, each of which took charge of one set of movements at a time and managed the exchange of responsibility several times. But the 20th century saw a steady drift in value creation toward larger retailers, and they, with the help of technology, have the capacity to coordinate all of these flows themselves, either by viewing stock movements throughout the value chain via electronic connections or by physically taking charge of the product from the factory gate.

Connecting the chain

A whole raft of information technologies, including telecommunications, electronic point-of-sale (POS) systems, and electronic data interchange, has come to underpin retailers' ability to operate these four value creation levers from one end of the value chain to the other, and to do so at speed and scale. As a result, retailers today can take advantage of relatively fixed central costs to operate ever-larger networks of stores, and they can make better-informed decisions more quickly.

Telecommunications

With so much focus on computing power and data storage facilitating the flow of information in the value chain, it is easy to forget the early role that improvements in telecommunications have played in retailing efficiency, linking producers, head office buyers and merchandisers, distribution centers, and stores. Today it would be unthinkable to run, say, a 50-store chain without economical modern telecommunications technology in support. Indeed, the data transfer that now takes place using fixed-wire and wireless telecommunications links is integral to almost every retail business. Bandwidth capacity has increased massively; what used to take minutes or hours on a dedicated, expensive, fixed-line link now happens in fractions of a second through handheld devices, improving all retail processes that benefit from quick access to information, but particularly those related to the physical movement of stock.

But telephone lines have only relatively recently been capable of carrying data at scale; these first advances were through analog voice transmission. And though from today's perspective, analog placed obvious cost and capacity constraints on how much, and how fast, information could move around networks, especially when simple reporting and data transformations had to be performed manually by clerks and accountants, voice communication represented an extraordinary advance in itself.

Very early on, the largest retailers quickly saw the commercial potential of telecommunications not only to speed the flow of information through their supply chains but also as a shopping channel. In 1909, when Selfridges first opened on Oxford Street in London, it advertised in *The Times* in terms that neatly summarized its view of the retailer's mission and emphasized the newest of new technology—the telephone:

> What infinite care in selection, expert judgment in buying, enterprise in finding new fields for purchases, absolute straightforwardness in describing commodities, continual supervision of every department, consideration for the customer's time—what all this can do to aid success has been done at Selfridges'. Moreover, certain entirely new methods, all designed for the increased comfort of the buyer, have been introduced; not the least among these being a system which will permit comfortable shopping by telephone.[4]

Colorful advertising promoted the new telephone system, which promised to connect the consumer to all the departments in the store, but it was a system only for the richest customers.[5]

In practice, customers did not leap at this opportunity. Access to telephones remained relatively restricted for some time, and in any case a voice call was really only useful for people who knew what they wanted to order in the first place. In due course, telephone ordering did become part of mail-order retail, but that in turn was viable only after the arrival of cheaper printing and postal costs. Progress was slow. By 1934, the chairman of Ericsson Telephones was saying to shareholders, perhaps rather optimistically, "There is still considerable scope for further telephone expansion, particularly among private users, and it may be that some of our traffic congestion will be relieved by a judicious 'shopping by telephone'."[6] As telephone shopping gradually gathered pace, its momentum depended upon cheaper and more widespread access to the technology among customers, along with the scale efficiency of having dedicated call centers in place of store employees to deal with customers.

What we would recognize as the modern call center first arrived in the 1960s, with the deployment of private branch exchanges to deal with large numbers of customers (although retailers were generally slower than financial-services companies to embrace these opportunities). In time, important enabling computer technology emerged: the automatic call distributor helped ensure that the most appropriate employee responded to each incoming call (by using an algorithm to determine which agent received which call). Call centers have since developed into highly sophisticated entities that use, among other technologies, data entry and speech recognition software that enable computers to provide initial-level customer support and, of course, digitize customer input.

In practice, though, retailers were less successful in generating sales from remote call centers than in using them for the provision of customer assistance.[7] In comparison, the effect of new customer-facing digital technologies is all the more striking. For example, by 2011, the volume of sales made over the Internet in the United Kingdom—the most advanced major market for digital retailing by proportion of sales—had grown to more than six times that in nondigital mail order.[8]

Electronic point-of-sale systems

The technology most associated with retail, and the best-known accelerator of information transfer between participants in the value chain and hence the efficient flow of physical goods, is that of the Uniform Product Code, or bar code. These codes, which capture real-time data about items as they flow through the supply chain, were originally designed to improve customer service and reduce labor costs by accelerating the checkout process.[9] But the technology's potential to collect more data and transfer it cheaply and quickly was soon grasped by retailers and manufacturers alike; for the first time, both parties were able to gather meaningful information about what was selling, where it was selling, and, in the most basic sense, who was buying it. Consumers, by contrast, were initially wary of the 59 black and white bars. According to an article published in the *New York Times* in 2009 to mark the 35th anniversary of the technology's introduction,[10] many shoppers refused to buy bar-coded products for fear they would be cheated at the checkout because the items did not carry regular price labels.

These days, retailers have the ability to track a *single* item—a can of drink, say—through the value chain from the moment it comes off the production line to the moment it is scanned at the supermarket checkout, *and* to receive that information in a form that readily allows its manipulation and analysis, thereby delivering a leap in operational efficiency that extends way beyond the checkout process. All retail selection and merchandising is part of a big set of feedback loops: "Shall we sell bicycles? Let's try. Ah, it appears we can't sell bicycles. Cancel all the outstanding orders!" Electronic POS systems essentially represent a radical improvement in the quality of those loops, keeping retailers and manufacturers better informed about what is selling where, and when; helping manufacturers to support and retailers to make decisions about preselection; and aiding the efficient physical movement of stock.[11]

One member of the team that introduced the bar code to the US grocery industry estimated that it had a clear upward effect on sales of between 10 and 12 percent and reduced store operating costs by an average of 1 to 2 percent.[12] Assuming a gross margin of 25 percent, the sales increase was in fact worth more than the cost saving.

Retailers today have discovered ways to improve the labor efficiency of the bar code still further. Some have built several scanners into cash registers (till units) to help ensure the code is always read with a single swipe, while the German discount grocery chain Aldi has increased the length of the bar codes on its private-label products for the same purpose. Such time saving counts in a business where store employees manage a range of tasks, freeing them up for more value-adding activities, such as moving stock. More recent experiments have included introducing automatic scanning systems using 3D sensors to read bar codes as items pass on a belt through a portal.

These kinds of enhancements are nevertheless limited to the amount of information that bar codes and their linear pictogram can contain, namely eight- or 13-character references. By contrast, the quick response (QR) code not only is quickly read, as its name implies, but also can compress far more information into its small square of black and white dots. A Web address, say, can be easily embedded as a database reference. Another recent innovation is radio frequency identification (RFID), which uses radio waves to transfer data to a reader from an electronic tag attached to a particular item. In a store, a shopper would not be required to have purchases scanned individually but would simply leave them in a shopping cart or basket and walk through, say, an RFID reader gateway that would pull all the requisite information off the tags before the customer proceeded to payment. The potential of these new technologies is discussed further in Chapter 3.

Electronic data interchange

The principal processing benefits of the bar code arose from its use at the point of sale. Earlier in the value chain, electronic data interchange (EDI) has been of comparable importance in extracting value from the preselection and physical movement of stock, delivering a similar leap in the speed of data transfer, the integrity and hence accuracy of the data, and cost-efficiency. Whereas the bar code enabled retailers and manufacturers to make sense of the effects of their decisions through retrospective analysis, EDI, introduced in retail in the mid-1980s, helped them transact among themselves more efficiently, for it is the means by which supplier and purchaser can have simultaneous recognition of shipments, deliveries, invoices, and payments.[13]

By using agreed-upon message standards, EDI enables the instant transfer of data without human intervention. It works because of shared protocols; only with these is it possible for, say, an electronic invoice issued by the systems of the vendor to give rise to an order-processing route in the systems of the purchaser. For retailers, which must typically manage many thousands or even hundreds of thousands of different data flows across their assortments of goods, it is a core technology. It has transformed category management (the way modern retailers organize to perform their preselection function) and is now also crucial in planning and tracking the movement of stock.

EDI also reduces errors by enforcing a high degree of discipline about master file data, the items in a computer system that are permanent or at least are not changed by any given transaction. (For a retailer, such data would include supplier names and addresses and the precise specifications of a given stock keeping unit, usually shortened to SKU.) EDI establishes clear conventions about the naming and numbering of different items, as well as consistency in referring to each of them and to different stores or departments. Because of this, EDI has significantly reduced the capacity for processing errors. In the preselection function of larger modern retailers, the consistency of the master data has improved the coordination of the ordering, production, delivery, and sales cycles for each product.

Knowing what you know

It is a truism that insight is more valuable than information, which is in turn more valuable than mere data. And it is also true that many retailers collect far more data than they can possibly use. But this should not mask the importance of developments in data storage, retrieval, and analysis, initially in the form of preset reports and increasingly in the form of individually generated inquiries.

Data storage and retrieval

We can trace over several decades the development of greater storage capacity, faster access, and better integration and connectivity in the systems that support retail. But to understand the importance of this development, we have to remember a world in which, to start with, virtually every data-recording operation involved significant manual input and data transfers were either complex and slow or else accomplished by more manual input. So while the underlying nature of retail remained the same (after all, retailers continued to add value through the same four intermediary functions), greater storage capacity and faster retrieval have made the industry more cost-efficient. What is more, by accelerating information transfer and decision-making processes, they have made it possible to coordinate activities across many hundreds or even thousands of different sites.

This process was, of course, gradual. When the first electronic data systems were introduced into retailers in the 1950s and 1960s, they were automating individual elements of information flow, not encompassing entire processes in the way to which we are accustomed today. For example, distribution of goods from the manufacturer could be speeded up by using punched cards and large electronic computers to prepare delivery notes and update central stockholding quantities. Equally, a replenishment order from a store could be assembled more quickly by reducing the time store personnel took to specify what they required.[14] These solutions represented advances in efficiency as well as in speed and accuracy, but for management analysis and decision making, retailers still relied on time-consuming, largely manual processes. The real value of electronic data processing in retail was to depend upon much more powerful systems for data retrieval and manipulation, and more and more frequent data transfer cycles. Self-evidently, sales and stock figures that are updated every hour are more useful guides to management supervision and decision making than figures that change only daily or weekly.

Thus, even though progressively more reporting could be carried out automatically, the link between retailers' operational systems and decision-support systems in the early decades of electronic data processing was weak. It was eventually strengthened by a new generation of computers and databases that could be interrogated by customized routines, running reports for users based on powerful query languages that could answer increasingly specific questions—best-sellers, for instance, or sales figures presented by one or more taxonomic criteria. Thus, sales could be analyzed by product division, store, and region, but also by size, color, or price point; outstanding orders could be sorted by delivery month or supplier; stockholding by site, age, or markdown percentage. Though a considerable advance, these reports still required specialist personnel to write the queries. It is only relatively recently that more powerful application software packages have been developed to allow users to ask their questions directly of their data. This kind of functionality began to emerge only in the 1980s, and it remains pivotal to data analysis in retail today.

An example of the hardware that could produce these customized reports was IBM's AS/400, a midrange computer that enabled retailers to use the systems that collected accounting and stock control data to produce reports such as best-sellers by various criteria or sales analyses by different combinations of store or product type. But, mostly, reports produced by computers such as these could only look backward, at historic data, and only through lenses (prepared report formats) designed for them by colleagues in the IT department or by an external vendor. The reports were not the actual underlying data, but abstractions from it.

Another reason for working only with data summaries or abstractions, besides constraints on computing and storage capacity, was simply to control how much data was transferred, and hence the costs of transfer. Without integrated systems (those in which computers can share information, as in client-server systems)[15] and fast telephone connections, heavy data users such as retailers had to contend with cumbersome, costly processes for copying, moving and storing data. In contrast, the most recent developments in information technology offer a world in which, in effect, the user gathers and keeps information at hand all the time. With "in-memory" computing, data is held continuously in the working memory of the computer.

For retail businesses, this change in data storage and retrieval systems has far-reaching implications. Depending always upon the underlying quality and completeness of the data fed into the system,[16] the retailer is able to work and react in nearly real time. That has significant repercussions not just for analytic capacity but also for the business uses to which data can be put.

Digital analysis

The ability to store and access data at scale has been the foundation for increasingly sophisticated analysis. Integrated systems can produce standard reports (sales by department, or top sellers versus slowest sellers), but some of the most dramatic advances have come from software packages that sit "on top" of the main databases. Usually known as enterprise resource planning (ERP) systems, they capture the fundamental processes involved in the ordering, receiving, storage, distribution, and sale of stock (and often much more).

One of the most significant advances in analysis has been the spreadsheet, a prime demonstration of how a data management tool can deliver huge efficiency gains to retailing tasks. Most planners and merchandisers now inhabit a world of digital spreadsheets, but only 40 years or so ago, most retailers still worked on large paper worksheets, pencil and eraser in hand.

The spreadsheet became widely known in the late 1970s and early 1980s, owing in large part to the VisiCalc program, which included most of the key features of modern spreadsheets with their referenced cells, formula lines, and automatic recalculation. Crucially, it enabled the user to set up calculations in a manner that was visually consistent with the familiar world of paper and pencil.[17] It was first deployed on the Apple II computer in 1979 (two years before landing on the IBM PC) and is widely considered to have been responsible for the success of that particular desktop computer.

Following the development of Lotus 1–2–3 and the inclusion of the Excel program in the Microsoft Office software suite, the spreadsheet became an everyday piece of technology. Today its importance has not diminished as it continues to improve the decision-making capabilities of individual retail managers and employees in their tasks of managing the supply chain and organizing the physical movement of stock, as well as improving efficiency in category management by aiding preselection.

In the world of fashion retail, for example, where merchandisers must work top-down from a total sales budget to quantify and sequence specific orders by category, style, color, and size, the introduction of the spreadsheet made a huge difference to what was feasible for a small team. Keeping track of buying and allocating decisions no longer needed an army of merchandise clerks. Indeed, spreadsheet software can be said to have played a vital part in the shift from a long-standing business model with two main seasons of individual styles (typically, spring/summer and autumn/winter) to one with four, six, or even more seasons, making the preselected merchandise increasingly appealing to the customer.

The spreadsheet also serves as an excellent example of a more general trend in the development of data analysis in retail and other data-intensive businesses: that more and more computing power and analytic flexibility are being provided directly to business executives. That trend reflects the history of computing, of course, in that successive generations of programming languages have become more and more powerful abstractions of the underlying binary operations of the processor itself. Few programmers now understand the finer points of machine code.

A succession of evolutions

A combination of advances in data transfer, storage, and analysis in the digital era has given rise to the development of a new set of analytic tools. The magnetic strips on loyalty cards, combined with sharp reductions in the cost of data storage and processing and some smart mathematics, have enabled retailers to collect purchase data from customers and subject it to comprehensive segmentation and correlation analysis, and to tailor marketing communications with unprecedented precision. This degree of specificity and customer insight again creates value, not just in the retailer's immediate decision-making and operations but also in enabling it to monetize technology-led insights by making highly targeted promotions available to manufacturers that wish to fund them.

But we are moving ahead of ourselves. Before the digital era, the general effect of technological advances was to improve the productivity of retailers' operations, helping them efficiently transfer large quantities of goods and operate larger stores stocked more comprehensively with well-selected goods, all thanks to greater information transparency. The information gave them a considerable advantage in dealing with suppliers, too. The better retailers' insight into sales, the stronger their basis for negotiation. But though many of the new technologies were presented as revolutionary in their time, they did not, in fact, change the way retailers competed with one another or, importantly, served customers. The retail stores of the late 20th century were not so different from those of 50 or

100 years earlier. And this use of technology was relatively generic. Essentially, many retailers acquired the same software and went through similar process changes.

The same was true of the first wave of e-commerce in the late 1990s, although it was expected *really* to shake things up. But for the mass of retailers through the first decade of the new millennium, e-commerce was mainly another silo of systems, with limited real integration into their core, store-driven business models.

Granted, retailers did have to change their mindsets, processes, and organizations to capture value, and the changes were often complex, challenging, and time-consuming for leaders. But while each change was important, none led to wholesale transformation. Instead, a succession of evolutions played out over many years, so retailers that committed to pay the "new price to play" in terms of systems and capabilities had a chance to catch up with the early leaders. And all the while, the cost declines and performance improvements were in the *existing* architecture. The digital era promises something quite different.

Notes

1. The elevators came from the Exposition Universelle of 1867 and really were cutting-edge technology for their time.
2. For our general purposes, integration can relate both to a retailer's internal systems and to electronic data interchange with suppliers and distributors. The net effect is the same: a radical increase in speed, data integrity, and cost-efficiency in the management of information flows.
3. It is one thing to decide to offer fresh cheese, and another to decide which varieties to sell.
4. *The Times* (London), March 22, 1909, display advertisement on p. 6. Telephone shopping had already been pioneered by Harrods.
5. By the end of that month, *The Times* featured a further advertisement from Selfridges, describing a fictional incident in which a husband and wife return to their Chelsea house from the Continent, only to find all of their possessions

missing. They are comforted by Selfridges' ability to take and fulfill a complex order on the same day by telephone. *The Times*, March 31, 1909.

6. *The Times*, April 27, 1934, p. 23.

7. See, for instance, *Retail Week* from August 14, 2009, reporting that DSGi, the leading UK consumer electronics retailer, receives 34,000 calls a day to its contact center. Joanna Perry, "Retailers shaking up contact centres."

8. See *UK Remote Shopping Report 2011*, table 2, Verdict Research, December 21, 2012.

9. US Food Fair asked experts at the Drexel Institute of Technology in Philadelphia to accelerate the checkout process. The first patent was filed in 1952 but used a bull's-eye design of concentric circles of different intensity. The distinctive bar code design came later. One of the co-inventors subsequently explained that he had played with Morse code in sand on the beach, converting dots and dashes into longer and variably thick bars.

10. Gerry C. Shih, "Game changer in retailing, bar code is 35," *New York Times*, June 25, 2009, http://www.nytimes.com/2009/06/26/technology/26barcode.html?_r=0), accessed January 23, 2013.

11. Bill Selmeier, *Spreading the Barcode* (self-published and available at lulu.com, 2008).

12. Ibid note 11.

13. Andrew Pollack, "Technology: Doing business by computer," *New York Times*, July 10, 1986, http://www.nytimes.com/1986/07/10/business/technology-doing-business-by-computer.html, accessed January 23, 2013.

14. Some very clear descriptions of this kind of system are available at the Museum of London's website. See "The Sainsbury Archive: Story of a supermarket," Museum of London, http://www.museumoflondon.org.uk/Collections-Research/Research/Your-Research/SainsburyArchive/, accessed January 23, 2013.

15. In the simplest sense, this terminology applies to all those situations in which two or more computers can talk to each other, so that one (or both) can provide resources to the other. Contrast this arrangement with a member of staff having to take a physical copy of data on a magnetic storage medium from one place to another so that a further copy can be made and used by a second computer.

16. See an interview with Jim Hagemann Snabe, co-CEO of SAP, *Financial Times*, June 1, 2011.

17. Or in a phrase that became generically applied to a host of modern software packages, what you see is what you get (WYSIWYG).

Chapter 3

Game-Changing Technologies

Co-authored with Roger Roberts

In Japan, the audience at a top fashion show can buy the latest outfits the very moment they are modeled on the catwalk, thanks to a mobile application that sends real-time, close-up pictures of the clothes along with links for making a purchase.[1] In the United Kingdom, one retailer collects no fewer than 1.5 billion new items of data every month—and can analyze them meaningfully.[2] Its segmentation model, for example, now differentiates between 3,000 groups of customers, up from six previously. And in the United States, a pizza delivery company can cope with huge spikes in demand during the Super Bowl without installing extra IT capacity.

These are examples of three preeminent, parallel, and mutually reinforcing trends that will define the digital era of retailing: mobility, measurability, and agility. The availability of technology everywhere—in stores, at home, on the go—will power mobility: consumers can consider what to buy and make the purchase anywhere, anytime. Far more activities in the value chain will be measured more accurately, not least consumer behavior. Agility will come from further development of cloud computing, which allows companies to develop systems—so often the roadblock that slows progress in improving business processes or pioneering new business models—with speed and productivity.

The technology behind these trends will help retailers improve their processes and contrive new experiences for consumers to a degree previously unimaginable. But the technology is also ushering in new competitors and empowering customers. Consequently, it will shift the basis of competition in the industry. Retailers do not control the pace of this change. Whether or not they are ready, a revolution—a real one this time—is coming.

Revolution

As Chapter 2 described, technology has been the catalyst for change throughout retailing's history. More recently and more specifically, the driving force has been *information* technology, starting with the rise of data processing in the retail back office during the 1960s and 1970s, continuing with the deployment of increasingly capable point-of-sale (POS) systems that enabled transaction and payment capture in the 1980s, and becoming more sophisticated with the rise of client-server business process systems and enterprise resource planning in the 1990s. These systems—for enterprise-wide accounting, supply chain management, merchandising, and warehouse and transportation management—were pioneering advances, certainly, but the change they represented was essentially incremental, rather than revolutionary.

This time around, we are dealing not with incremental change but with a transformation embracing each retail stakeholder and thus the entire industry. The things that producers, retailers, and consumers can do, and the relationships among these three parties, are being reconfigured. Simply stated, technology now enables all the parties to engage in tasks that only recently were beyond them.

This transformation is possible because of technological advances enabled by a series of innovations hatched in the laboratory and put into mass production by technology providers around the world. These advances are occurring, apparently inexorably, in three main areas. The first is computer processing power, which has risen exponentially via the development of low-cost semiconductor chips. The second area is networking, which occurred first via wired broadband connections and then wirelessly. Finally, in the area of data storage, the capacity available both to end-user devices and to large data centers has vastly expanded as unit costs have fallen.

Computing

Computing has improved in performance, as famously predicted in Moore's law. The Intel pioneer Gordon Moore forecast in 1965 that the number of transistors on a single processor chip would double every two years, as it duly did, even as prices fell rapidly (Exhibit 3.1).

At a simple level, this means that the phones in our pockets have capacity to process software instructions far exceeding that of the largest business computers of the 1970s. The research of professors Erik Bryjnolfsson and Andrew McAfee at MIT's Sloan School of Management illustrates this impact at a macro level. They analyzed the prices of assets in the US

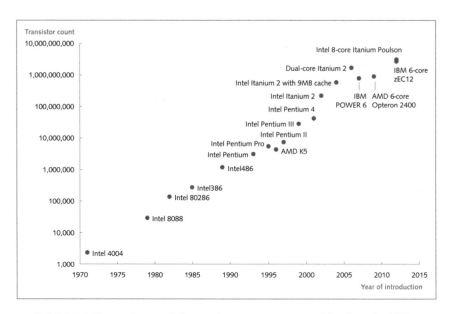

Exhibit 3.1 Dramatic growth in transistors per processor chip since the 1970s.
Source: Intel, AMD, IBM.

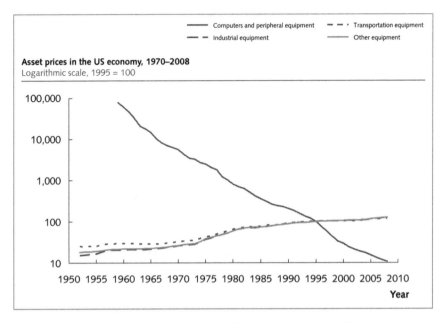

Exhibit 3.2 Dramatic drop in cost of processing over past 50 years.
Source: MIT Center for Digital Business (2010).

economy (adjusted for quality or performance) and found that, when indexed and plotted together, the costs of most resources—manufacturing plant and transportation equipment, for example—moved at a similar pace, whereas the relative cost of computing equipment plummeted (Exhibit 3.2).

As a resource for delivering economic output, IT has grown so much faster than other resources that it is difficult to represent the figures on the same chart. This is true not only in the United States (Exhibit 3.3) but also in almost every other developed and emerging market around the world.

Information and the technology that makes it useful are together becoming the primary resources that drive competition across many sectors of the economy. However, not everyone will benefit equally. If the

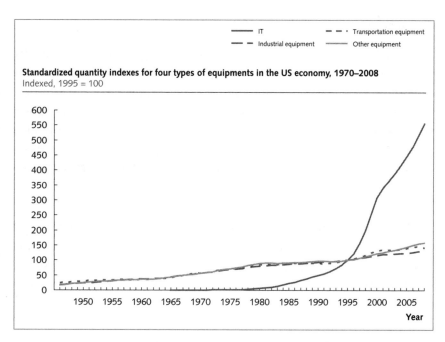

IT — — · Transportation equipment
— — Industrial equipment ——— Other equipment

Standardized quantity indexes for four types of equipments in the US economy, 1970–2008
Indexed, 1995 = 100

Exhibit 3.3 Soaring investment in IT adjusted for performance.
Source: MIT Center for Digital Business (2010).

patterns seen in other industries prevail, the performance spread between retail's leaders and laggards in the use of information will grow.[3]

For retailers, the growth in inexpensive computing power allows the use of information to move out of the back office and into the store—as well as into the homes and pockets of consumers. Instant analysis can help store managers react in real time to trends and shifts in customers' behavior. Mobile devices can run software applications ("apps") that render images of a person's house fitted out with new furniture or take pictures of new clothes and overlay them onto personal photographs. Heavy-duty computing can even enable a friend, or even a nosy neighbor, to photograph items in your house and then match the images online to find out where to buy the same things. Less intrusively, apps can take your location and shopping list and find the stores offering the best combination of price and convenience.

Networking

The networking technology pioneer Robert Metcalfe described the impact of the growth in networks operating on standard protocols, the most important of which is the Internet, as being exponential: the size of a network (the number of unique connections among network users) grows with the square of the number of users connected.[4] If the value of a network equals its size, as argued by Metcalfe, this implies that the value of adding a new connection point to a network is proportional to the network's size (Exhibit 3.4).

Put simply, the more people connected to the network, the more useful mobile phone, social media, or payment transaction networks—to name but a few—become. Thus, making big networks bigger is highly valuable, and their value continues rising as new services are created and more data is shared.

And the number of Internet endpoints is growing fast. Technology provider Cisco predicted in 2012 that by 2016 there will be three Internet-connected devices per capita worldwide, up from one in 2011. The density is even higher in the most developed economies. Cisco also forecast in 2012 that Internet protocol traffic will grow in aggregate by 29 percent a year until 2016. In addition, the amount of traffic that travels wirelessly

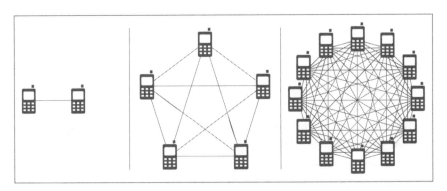

Exhibit 3.4 Metcalfe's law.

from devices to the core network is exploding. A set of wireless data innovations known as Long-Term Evolution (LTE) technology is making its way into the fourth-generation (4G) networks deployed by mobile providers, bringing more efficient use of the airwaves to deliver data. Cisco notes that mobile data traffic is growing at rates similar to those of the wired Internet in the boom years of the late 1990s, and that by 2016 the amount of data moving wirelessly from networked devices will exceed that traveling over wired access networks. For retailers and consumers, such changes are triggering all sorts of new uses for mobile devices. Retailers, for example, can stream on-demand training videos to store employees' handheld devices for the employees to watch at home or while commuting to work. Households with wired kitchens can assemble shopping lists based on usage and buying patterns, and then find the lowest-cost sources for restocking the shelves. Apps can advise on diet choices that meet our health goals, perhaps encouraging us to try new foods or ways of preparing them. Simple interfaces, via touch or voice, are making it easier for older or technophobic users to try out the same capabilities as everyone else, or allow those with limited mobility the chance to shop or interact with store employees via video.

Storage

Capacity to store information in cheap and stable ways has advanced at incredible rates, in multiple storage media and on connected devices, and in the vast data centers that host corporate and consumer IT services (Exhibit 3.5).

Storage media are becoming denser, so the physical size of storage devices is shrinking as capacity grows, and their cost is falling. The software to manage that storage and make it widely accessible and secure likewise has improved rapidly. Researchers at IDC note that 2.7 zettabytes of information will be stored in 2012, replicated across many, many devices—an increase of 48 percent over 2011.[5] A zettabyte is 1×10^{21} bytes, or one trillion gigabytes (Exhibit 3.6). We are creating and capturing information on a scale that is hard to grasp.

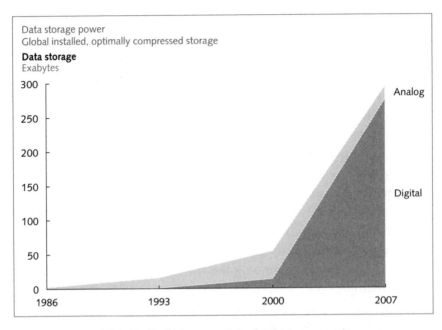

Exhibit 3.5 Explosive growth in data storage capacity.
Source: Martin Hilbert and Priscila López, "The world's technological capacity to store, communicate, and compute information," *Science* 332, no. 6025 (April 2011).

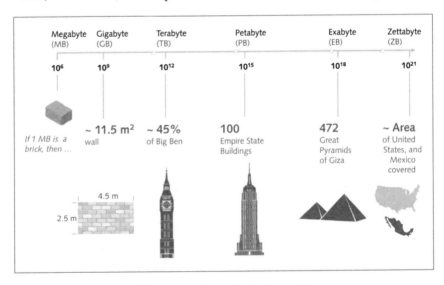

Exhibit 3.6 From megabytes to zettabyte.
Source: McKinsey Global Institute.

The trend is not merely continuing, it is accelerating as many more types of data are digitized and more of this data is retained for analysis and "mining." For users of PCs, tablet computers, and smartphones, flash memory has made tremendous capacity available at low cost and with modest power consumption. This capacity enables an enormous range of apps to be downloaded and innovative forms of content to be consumed. For example, video can be integrated into digital catalogs with live links to the Buy button. Customers can capture, upload, and share images and videos about their shopping experiences, good and bad. And retailers can gather detailed information about how, what, when, and why we buy.

All that sharing of data, of course, raises the question of trust. In return for all the information, consumers are likely to demand some control over when, how, and by whom it is used. Earning the trust of customers will be vital if retailers are also to earn their loyalty. Therefore, we expect retailers to become more open about what data they retain and how they use the data, and to explain more fully how their use of customer data helps create value for consumers as well as the retailers' own businesses.

The next era of technology change

So far, retailers are only starting to understand the opportunities presented by their data assets. Essentially, though, the advances in computing, networking, and storage hardware and software make it possible to deliver data in new ways to mobile devices, measure all the activities in business processes, assess more accurately the behavior of consumers, and use disparate sources of data while scaling capacity up and down. In other words, the advances power mobility, measurability, and agility.

Mobility

Imagine it is the late 1990s. Picture a tech-savvy tourist indulging in a pre-Christmas shopping spree through New York City. Sophisticated as she is, we find she has equipped herself with several electronic devices: a mobile phone, which enables her to call friends and tell them about her purchases and discoveries; a fancy digital camera; headphones that connect to her portable compact-disc player; a weekly timetable on her handheld PDA; and a portable GPS navigation unit, enabling her to find the shortest route through the streets of Manhattan. Along with this gear, she is toting a 280-page, two-pound guide to the New York City Christmas shopping season. In short, she is burdened with heavy, bulky, and complex equipment.

Today, of course, those gadgets, the book, and all of the information they provide are readily available in a single piece of equipment not much larger than a chocolate bar: a high-end mobile phone or tablet computer. Without a doubt, the arrival of advanced mobile devices such as smartphones and tablets has empowered and simplified the lives of millions of consumers around the world.

What is changing

In the case of highly capable mobile devices, the innovation lies less in refining an existing functionality and more in combining a multitude of functionalities into a single, handheld device. Many basic features of mobile devices, such as phone and text communications, Internet access, and camera and entertainment options, already existed well before the arrival of smartphones, with each offering some clear and independent value to the consumer. Integrating all of these functionalities into a single unit—a trend known as device convergence—makes the mobile phone the one accessory that most people carry with them all the time (Box 3.1).

Device convergence has inspired software developers to create a multitude of applications that link the phone to other services via the Internet, turning it into a multifunctional tool for commerce. And all the while, mobile performance is improving thanks to the three fundamental technology forces described earlier. With the advent of 4G LTE networks and hot-spot-based Wi-Fi, data transfer rates are increasing, while coverage is

Box 3.1 Convergence at a glance

Definition

Convergence is the combining of multiple information technologies and uses such as computing, communication networks, and media content consumption into one device.

Background

Smartphones and tablets are bringing many functions that used to be provided by independent devices (e.g. cameras, PCs, music players, gaming devices) into a single tool. Five enablers—the faster mobile networks providing links to the Internet at desktop speeds, cloud computing, sensor and scanning technology, near-field communication (NFC) technology for short-range data exchange, and advances in personal geolocation—are combining to put a host of functions and activities at the consumer's fingertips (Exhibit 3.7). The following applications are just examples:

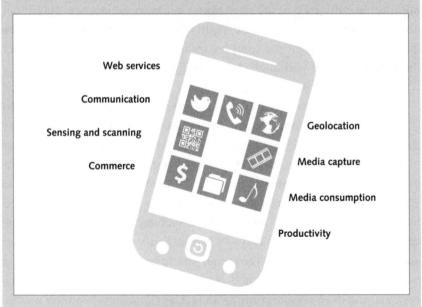

Exhibit 3.7 Multifunctionality of mobile devices.

- **Communication**—telephony, texting, e-mail, instant messaging/chat, and Web conferencing
- **Web services**—Web searches, e-commerce, social networks, micro-blogs (e.g. Twitter)
- **Sensing and scanning**—sound/voice recognition, bar code and QR code scanning
- **Commerce**—mobile payments via NFC, self-checkout, loyalty card management and reward redemption
- **Geolocation**—mapping, route planning, geotagging, location-based interaction
- **Media capture**—photography, video recording, audio recording
- **Media consumption**—games, music, video (viewed on the screen or projected digitally to a convenient surface)
- **Productivity**—document creation, editing, and sharing; storage and synchronization of files across devices; contact management

approaching ubiquity. At the same time, smartphones' storage capabilities are mushrooming, low-cost and highly powerful processors enable the devices to handle multiple complex tasks, and advanced screens render the visual interface with high-definition fidelity.

As mobile devices have improved, usage and penetration have soared (Exhibit 3.8). In the United States, 40 percent of all mobile phones sold by the third quarter of 2011 were smartphones—more than double their share in 2009. And according to the technology research firm Gartner, smartphones and tablets combined make up 70 percent of all devices sold in 2012.[6] Growth in mobile usage outpaces PC-based use of the Internet, and mobile apps have already surpassed PC Web browsing in terms of time spent per user (81 minutes versus 74 in a 2011 survey). For many on-the-go activities, as well as some in the home, smartphones and tablets are taking over tasks formerly performed with PCs, cameras, handheld game systems, and even remote controls. In fact, as consumers use their mobile devices to tap the Internet, the main use of these devices is shifting away

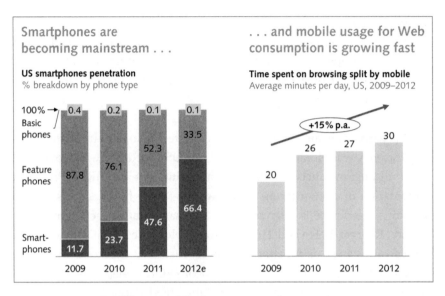

Exhibit 3.8 Mobile device usage and penetration.
Source: Yankee Group (2012), McKinsey iConsumer Initiative.

from voice communication. People are using them instead for texting, location-based services, and commerce.

For retailers, this trend is important, because the devices are empowering customers by readily providing them with more information than consumers have ever had in the past. They use a smartphone to find local deals, scan prices in a store in order to compare the store's price with other prices (a trend dubbed "showrooming"), check user-generated or professional product reviews in the aisle, and seek opinions from family and friends before deciding to buy. The subject of consumer empowerment is discussed in detail in Chapter 4.

Not all of the power is flowing to consumers. Innovative retailers are using mobile devices as a productivity and efficiency tool, to support sales staff or manage the upstream supply chain. The devices will influence many retail operations: the tracking and tracing of goods en route or inventory in stock, and the in-store procedures for checkout and product return. They might even lead to the creation of virtual "stockless stores," where phone-equipped consumers can scan items in a virtual display and have them shipped home or prepared for pickup at a commuter transit station. In South Korea and China, some retailers are already experimenting with the idea (see Chapter 4).

One early innovator in the use of mobile technology to improve retailing efficiency was Home Depot. In 2011, the US-based home improvement and building products retailer began rolling out its FIRST Phone, a combination of a smartphone and a walkie-talkie. FIRST stands for the functions the device is intended to enable sales staff to perform: "Find, Inquire, Respect, Solve and Thank."[7] To enable those activities, the device carries out a host of functions, such as customer checkout, inventory management, voice-over-Internet protocol (VOIP) telephony, and label printing. One newspaper has compared the FIRST Phone to a Swiss Army knife for sales assistants.[8] Home Depot expects the devices will help its employees deliver enhanced customer service and more efficiently address questions and direct consumers to goods in the aisles. The *Wall Street Journal* reports that, as a direct result, the share of time sales associates spend effectively helping customers—rather than wasting time finding information on products or areas for which they don't have specialized expertise—increased to 53 percent by the end of 2011, up from roughly 40 percent in 2008.[9] According to the *Retail Technology Industry Guide*, the deployment represents the largest-ever rollout of mobile POS devices in retail.[10] Home Depot spent $64 million to develop the technology and purchase the first 30,000 devices, with an even larger rollout now under way (Exhibit 3.9).

What's next in mobile

Highly capable mobile devices have been around for a decade but gained widespread popularity only in the past five years or so. We are still at the very beginning of a megatrend that will continue, fundamentally reshaping retail. But we can begin to see glimpses of how this impact could manifest itself.

Exhibit 3.9 Home Depot's first phone device.
Source: Home Depot. This image of the FIRST phone is reproduced with permission from Homer TLC, Inc.

Technology is emerging in defense applications and in early proof-of-concept initiatives that take device experiences a step further. This is the world of augmented reality, which brings relevant information together with video or photos to add to the user's experience of the real world (Box 3.2). In early applications, this mostly means using a smart device's camera to capture real-time imagery, which is then overlaid with information or metrics gathered by linking the phone's location and digital recognition of the imagery it is capturing to online databases. For example, a sports fan at a game might point the camera at a player in an arena and see real-time statistics about that player's performance, or a shopper in a supermarket aisle could point the camera at a product to see health or sustainability ratings overlaid.

US defense contractor Raytheon has used augmented-reality technology on the battlefield, leading *The Economist* magazine to announce the arrival of the "droid war" era.[11] Indeed, the company has developed a mobile platform called Raytheon Android Tactical System, which combines digital maps with a list of comrades to create a platform offering

Box 3.2 Augmented reality at a glance

Definition
Augmented reality provides a view of a physical, real-world space in which electronic sensory inputs such as sound, video, graphics, or location data augment the user's experience of that environment in real time.

Overview
Augmented reality is related to virtual reality. But whereas virtual reality technologies immerse a user in a synthetic environment, with no sensory connection to the real world, augmented-reality technologies enable the user to see, hear, and touch the real world, with virtual objects superimposed upon or composited with the real world. They enhance, rather than replace, reality.

By magnifying people's senses and skills, augmented reality creates enhanced situational awareness and brings new data into a person's context without cutting off the person from that context. More advanced augmented-reality technologies (adding computer vision and object recognition, say) enable users to interact by sharing, sending, or transacting. Recent trends in augmented reality include image recognition and tracking, virtual product trials and social gaming, and the addition of location layers. All may be used to enhance retail and shopping experiences. For example, location layers are an increasingly popular tool for providing additional information on retail locations of interest, often based on online digital maps and location data.

Sources: Ronald T. Azuma, "A survey of augmented reality," *Presence: Teleoperators and Virtual Environments* 6, no. 4 (August 1997), pp. 355–85, available at http://www.cs.unc.edu/~azuma/ARpresence.pdf; Paul Sawers, "Augmented reality: The past, present and future," *The Next Web*, July 3, 2011, http://thenextweb.com/insider/2011/07/03/augmented-reality-the-past-present-and-future/.

Exhibit 3.10 Augmented reality for product displays.
Source: Blippar.

soldiers an augmented-reality app for smartphones, tablets, or any other smart mobile device. The app can overlay camera images with data from digital markers representing other members of a soldier's unit. In other words, the app creates a real-time graphic image of a soldier's surroundings, including the exact location of all comrades.[12]

Retailers are beginning to experiment with augmented-reality technology. The Blippar app, for example, was introduced in the United Kingdom in 2011. Users point their cameras at the Blippar logo, be it on a product in a supermarket, on a billboard, or in an advertisement in print media, to make the image spring to life with additional information (Exhibit 3.10).

Tokyo's N Building takes the concept even further. The windows on its facade are faced with supersized quick-response (QR) codes.[13] People on the street can point their mobile devices at the codes to open the building's website, where they can find shop information and downloadable coupons or make restaurant reservations without entering the building. In addition, the site overlays an image of the real building with virtual elements, so that tweets and blogs from employees inside are visible in speech bubbles, along with their avatars in constant motion (Exhibit 3.11).[14]

Exhibit 3.11 N Building in Tokyo and mobile sites showing tweets and avatars of people inside the building.
Source: Vimeo, http://vimeo.com/8468513#.[15]

The future role of augmented reality in retail remains uncertain, and many retailers are asking whether it truly has potential to add value for the customer or is a gimmick.[16] Nevertheless, intriguing possibilities arise. For example, augmented reality reduces the limitations of retailing without physical stores. Apps that use a computer's built-in camera or a smartphone camera to enable customers to create an augmented-reality image of a product (possibly, one day, in 3D) could further reduce the need to shop physically before making a purchase, especially if the buyer does not need to see or touch the object. Furniture retailer IKEA already offers an app that lets consumers stand in a room in their home and, by peering through their phone, place furniture into the picture.

Augmented reality could also change the nature of a manager's view of a store. A walk down the aisle could be augmented with information on sales rates or products that are out of stock or running short, or by the ability to see what shelf or display area is underperforming expectations. And there is no reason for the technology to be linked only to a mobile camera. Imagine also that an executive at headquarters could use live, in-store video feeds to "fly" through the aisle of a distant store and visualize what is selling in real time or the impact of a new promotional display.

This is a long way from simply hearing the sound of the cash register ringing up sales and knowing that your cash is flowing in and your goods are flowing out.

Technical challenges remain. GPS accuracy is limited, much software and device innovation must be undertaken before users become comfortable managing the interface, and social and legal conventions on when, how, and where to use such technology have yet to be established.[17] Yet progress to date does offer a peep into the future of mobile-enabled customer and commercial interactions.

Measurability

"I often say that when you can measure what you are speaking about, and express it in numbers, you know something about it; but when you cannot express it in numbers, your knowledge is of a meager and unsatisfactory kind; it may be the beginning of knowledge, but you have scarcely, in your thoughts, advanced to the stage of science, whatever the matter may be." So wrote William Thompson, later Lord Kelvin, the 19th-century physicist and engineer.

Retail is detail, and there are thousands of details to master on the way to becoming a leading merchant. As a business with vast numbers of stock-keeping units, transactions, and interactions making up the chain of commerce that brings goods to consumers, much of retail is measurable. But often those measures have been backward looking and aggregated, offering only overall sales trends for particular lines. Decision-making has been an art, and great merchants managed by gut instinct.

Nowadays, however, the integration of sensors into stores and mobile devices, the capacity to move the resulting data quickly almost anywhere on the planet, and the ability to aggregate, analyze, and act on this data are bringing retail closer to a science. Also, with apologies to Lord Kelvin, they are creating knowledge of a bountiful and much more satisfactory kind about what sells, who buys, and why and what can be done to sell more, realize higher prices, and waste less. As we have seen, retailers have long benefited from advances in computer processing power, data storage, and software development. The exploding power of technology and the vast amounts of information available to retailers are shifting this race into a new gear, however. We see this as the ability to measure everything— and the combination of advanced analytic techniques and huge stores of data is making it reality.

What is changing

Our work at McKinsey has identified the growth and use of "big data" as one of the small set of global forces that will drive tectonic economic shifts over the coming decade.[18] To use a common framing of the trend, big data means that the volume, velocity, and variety of data available to automated business processes, analysts, and decision-makers is growing amazingly fast (Box 3.3).

The use of big data creates value in important ways:

- It enables transparency, which can unlock value—for instance, by enabling visibility of inventory levels or customer flows in retail outlets.
- It can be used to expose variability and raise performance. As organizations create and store more transactional data in digital form, they can collect accurate, detailed performance information on everything from product inventories to sick days. They also can correlate these measures with external explanatory data, such as weather information.
- It can be used to segment populations according to ever-narrower criteria and to customize offerings and interactions. For example, promotions and coupons can be much more effective if more precisely targeted. This can extend to a "segment of one" (i.e. making inferences about individual behavior and preferences that allow for personalized offers).
- It enables the use of automated algorithms to support or even replace human decision-making. Sophisticated analytics can minimize risks and unearth valuable insights. By using data to tailor assortments, for example, retailers can take out bias and personal preferences of

Box 3.3 **Big data at a glance**

Definition
"Big data" refers to data for which the scale, distribution, diversity, and/or timeliness of delivery require the use of new technical architectures and analytics to enable insights that unlock new sources of value.

Overview
For a body of data to be classified as big data, rather than traditional analytics, it must have at least two of the following five characteristics:

* **Scale**—Massive, multi-petabyte data sets, designed to scale and collect more information
* **Distribution**—Data sources dispersed inside and outside the organization
* **Diversity**—Semi-structured, unstructured, or a combination of different data types
* **Timeliness**—Rapid and real-time capture of data, analytics, and decision-making
* **Analytics**—Adaptive and learning-based analytics that improve with the size of a data set and enable extraction of insights via innovative, collaborative, and iterative querying, filtering, correlation, and pattern finding.

merchants or supply planners and assure that they focus on the needs of customers as revealed in their transaction and behavior data streams.
* Data about the use of products can enable innovation in business models, products, and services. The emergence of real-time location data has led to the development of location-based mobile services, from navigation to people tracking.

The value at stake is enormous, and businesses and technology providers are racing to capture it. This study shows that in US retailing, use of big data could bring about an increase of between 20 and 30 percent in operating margin and drive growth of between 0.5 and 1 percent a year in total productivity.

What it means for retail

Historically, market and customer analytics were based on sampling, and inference from often small sample sizes and focus groups drove many decisions in consumer businesses. Financially, measures of profitability performance were less than fresh by the time managers got to see them, because, although sales were updated daily, profit and loss figures were drawn up monthly. Technology has the potential to change this story— and is already doing so in many ways.

Using big data, retailers can, for example, keep information on individual customers based on their shopping history, analyze patterns of needs and likes, and decide the most appropriate advertising. Add increased computing power and advances in software development, and retailers can conduct real-time analysis, so they can make tailored offers to customers while they are on the premises. Box 3.4 illustrates how accurately big data can be crunched today, while suggesting the challenges retailers must overcome before they can realize the potential of these tools and techniques.

These kinds of analytics are opening up new ways to drive sales and profits, but they will demand new tools, talent, and mindsets as well. Data-driven experimentation will enable all aspects of the retail experience and the presentation of goods to consumers to be tested and refined via analytics, much as search engines use thousands of daily experiments to refine the ways in which results are presented to users. Chapter 7 discusses in detail the new skills and capabilities that successful, digital-era retailers will require.

Box 3.4 A retailer identifies its pregnant customers

In a well-known case, a large North American retailer used big data to establish when customers were pregnant, long before the delivery date. This effort was not just an exercise in analytic wizardry, but rather a carefully planned response to the retailer's goal of forging customer relationships at a time when consumer needs undergo drastic changes. Having a baby is among the life experiences that can prompt significant changes in shopping habits and brand loyalties. That presents an opportunity for merchants, who often seek ways to shift long-standing shopping behavior and build new loyalty with customers.

The traditional approach to this opportunity has been to identify new parents following a birth, because birth records usually are publicly available. As a result, new parents are often bombarded with advertising and coupons. To gain a competitive advantage and be among the first to reach a new family with its message and offers, this retailer decided it wanted to know not only when a woman gave birth but also when she realized she was pregnant.

To answer this question, the company decided to look for patterns of shopping behavior associated with a new pregnancy. The retailer's analytics team studied its customer data and developed an algorithm for "pregnancy prediction" and for determining expected due dates, which it was able to do with a high accuracy rate. For example, the company reportedly determined that when female customers begin to buy supplements such as magnesium, zinc, or calcium, there is an 87 percent chance they are in their first 20 weeks of pregnancy, and when they start to acquire washcloths and hand sanitizers, they are close to giving birth.

Using these pregnancy scores to screen customers, the retailer identified about 25 products expectant parents buy, and it began to send coupons for baby products to households that they inferred included expectant women.

While it is not possible to separate out the impact of these data-driven techniques from many other factors, some journalists have attributed this retailer's greater than 50 percent sales growth from 2002 to 2010 at least partly to its success in attracting business from expectant mothers and their families.

The value at stake for retailers is clearly high, yet they must take care to ensure that the ability to deliver laser-targeted promotions does not seem so intrusive that it creates a backlash among the very customers whose business they are seeking to attract. We believe the value created for both consumers and retailers by careful targeting is large enough that the use of these tools will grow dramatically. However, the acceptance of these methods in different societies around the world may vary, creating challenges for retailers that hope to leverage their data analytics capabilities across borders.

Source: Charles Duhigg, "How companies learn your secrets," *New York Times*, February 16, 2012, http://www.nytimes.com/2012/02/19/magazine/shopping-habits.html?pagewanted=1&_r=3, accessed January 23, 2013.

What's next in data

Diversification of data sources is a long-running theme in retail. Initially, data came from sales reports and accounting processes. More recently, companies gathered data from POS and various types of business process software, including merchandising, supply chain management, and customer relationship management software. Next, Internet commerce enabled retailers to analyze all interactions with a website. Now the emergence of low-cost digital sensors, high-capacity wired and wireless networks, and software to aggregate, analyze, or visualize information is creating a world in which the physical and the digital are coming together. In other words, all events and attributes of the physical world can be captured, stored, and acted upon digitally. Goods can report their positions, freezer cabinets can let store staff know when it is time to restock, and customers' arrival at the store can be noted, all by real-time systems.

This so-called Internet of things (Box 3.5) will open up vast new sources of data. With chips attached to them, objects will be able to evaluate their own status or that of their environment, communicate with other objects (directly or via a central server), and even prompt a predefined set of actions based on their status evaluation. Smart refrigerators, for example, may be able to read the tags on items inside and give information such as shelf life, nutrients, and allergens, as well as interact with retailers, who may offer suggestions on recipes (in line with a household's dietary requirements perhaps, or making use of ingredients soon to pass their sell-by date) and additional ingredients needed. Consumers may even arrange for the retailer to provide automatic replenishment of items as they are consumed.

To create actionable information from all these new big data sources and streams, companies will require new forms of computing and processing. Dedicated analytic computing environments will be needed to search for real-time insights. New forms of visualization software and better user interfaces will help human analysts and decision-makers see patterns,

Box 3.5 Internet of things at a glance

Definition
The "Internet of things" refers to physical objects that have been embedded with sensors, have communications capabilities, and are linked through wired or wireless networks, often based on Internet protocols. Not only are data feeds provided from sensors of a vast number of types (e.g. light, heat, motion, pressure, pollution, and many, many more), but these may also be linked to actuators, or control loops, that take actions based on logic. A simple one is the temperature control for a room, but imagine if sensors and control logic could adjust multiple aspects of the store environment based on customer traffic and flow patterns—or even change prices dynamically.

Putting the Internet of things to work
More objects are being embedded with sensors and gaining the ability to communicate. Already, billions of such "smart objects" exist. Cisco predicts that, by 2020, 50 billion "things" will be connected to the Internet. IBM estimates that, by 2015, there will be one trillion connected devices.

The resulting information networks have the potential to foster new and improved business models, and to reduce costs and risks. Six types of applications are emerging (Exhibit 3.12). They fall into two broad categories: (1) information analysis and (2) automation and control.

Information and analysis	**Tracking behavior** Monitoring the behavior of persons, things, or data through space, time	**Enhanced situational awareness** Achieving real-time awareness of physical environment	**Sensor-driven decision analytics** Assisting human decision making through deep analysis, data visualization
Automation and control	**Process optimization** Automated control of closed (self-contained) systems	**Optimized resource consumption** Control of consumption to optimize resource use across network	**Complex autonomous systems** Automated control in open environments with great uncertainty

Exhibit 3.12 Emerging applications for the Internet of things.

Sources: M. Chui, M. Löffler, and R. Roberts, "The Internet of things," *McKinsey Quarterly*, no. 2 (2010), pp. 70–79; Cisco Systems, "The Internet of things," Cisco infographic, http://share.cisco.com/internet-of-things.html; Richard MacManus, "Cisco: 50 billion things on the Internet by 2020," *Read-Write*, July 17, 2011, infographic available at http://www.readwriteweb.com/archives/cisco_50_billion_things_on_the_internet_by_2020.php#more, accessed January 23, 2013.

assess options, and take action. The volume of data will also become the main driver of demand for data storage. So far, businesses have only scratched the surface; much further innovation from both technology providers and the analytics and IT teams of retailers will be needed to capture the potential.

In the retail sector, the Internet of things applies to daily operations in many ways. Radio frequency identification (RFID) chips improve inventory control or customer checkout (Box 3.6). In fact, retailing can be regarded as a leader in the development and deployment of RFID technology, beginning in the United States with Wal-Mart's store-level RFID pilot in 2004 and closely followed by Target and Albertsons.[19]

RFID technology was first used in retail to tag pallets and cases, but retailers have always understood that they would realize the technology's potential only when RFID tags were placed on individual items. In principle, this also allows for an automatic checkout of customers: they can simply walk through a scan zone that triggers the automatic calculation of the customer's basket. Of course, this will work only when all the goods on offer are tagged so they need not be scanned manually. To implement this idea, comprehensive stock preparation would be required, and the cost of RFID tags for very low-priced items would be disproportionate. These challenges explain why no full-scale supermarket trial has been made at the time of writing.

Nevertheless, in the menswear department of one of its outlets, a European department store operator made an intriguing experiment as early as 2005, putting RFID tags on every single item for sale in the department. The retailer asked its customers to make payment within the department, so that it could run a fully RFID-equipped store within a store. The experiment produced two results. First, the technology worked fine. Second, the dramatically shorter time required for taking inventory and the ability to trace missing items that had been left in the changing room or had fallen down the back of shelving units created a high level of transparency and reduced costs.

Box 3.6 The RFID story

An RFID system consists of a tag, a reader, and linkage that feeds data to systems that aggregate and enable its use. RFID was initially developed with retail and logistics applications in mind, the goal being the replacement of the bar code with a tag that can carry a richer range of information and can be reliably accessed via readers. While RFID tags themselves do not have IP addresses, readers do, so they provide the data link between RFID-tagged items and the Internet.

In 2004, Wal-Mart became the first to ship cases of consumer goods with RFID tags, with immediate success. The use of RFID tags greatly improved inventory control by assuring that the level of stock in the IT systems matches the actual stock on the floor and by tracking the movements of stock more closely, helping to avoid the costs of product shortages.

Today, RFID technology has come of age, and it is now normal for larger retailers such as Wal-Mart or Tesco to require suppliers to attach tags to pallets of products and sometimes to single units. Solutions providers have honed their expertise, while software vendors provide field-proven, retail-specific applications. Encouraged by the development of industry standards, companies such as Microsoft, Intel, Oracle, and IBM have made significant investments, putting interoperable RFID that allows multiple vendors' hardware and software solutions to work together within the grasp of many more retail users. Tags now come in a wide variety of shapes and sizes, enabling the tagging of any product at relatively low cost. The use of RFID chips is expected to grow exponentially, with the number of tags sold globally estimated to rise from 12 million in 2011 to 209 billion in 2021.

Source: James Manyika *et al.*, "Big data: The next frontier of innovation, competition, and productivity," McKinsey Global Institute, May 2011, http://www.mckinsey.com/insights/mgi/research/technology_and_innovation/big_data_the_next_frontier_for_innovation, accessed January 23, 2013.

Another application of the Internet of things is facial recognition by billboards, which enables more targeted advertising. As early as 2008, Japanese telecommunications company NTT tried out technology that counted the number of people in front of a billboard, analyzed whether they were looking at the advertisement, and, if they were looking, measured for how long. Today, some Japanese billboards have the technology to draw conclusions about the basic demographic profiles of passers-by, such as their sex and age bracket, and change displayed messages accordingly.[20]

In the future, billboards and video screens will have enough sensory intelligence and connectivity to identify a face with a quick search on Facebook or other social networking site. With that information, they can then display personalized messages or advertisements based on purchasing histories and social network data.

Widespread adoption of the Internet of things will take time, but the pace is accelerating, owing to improvements in the underlying technologies and standardization of communications protocols. In the near future, ever-smaller silicon chips for this purpose will acquire new capabilities, and costs will fall. For instance, standard RFID tags in the recent past were priced at 50 cents apiece; advanced tags using new materials are bringing the cost down to just 3 cents and could go below 1 cent, even with greater capabilities (Exhibit 3.13). And when billions of things are talking to one another, learning, and automating responses, then the only limitation left will be our imagination.

Agility

Information systems have often been the factor that slows progress when it comes to changing business processes or pioneering new business models. The development of systems has required long efforts to gather and refine requirements, to translate business needs into functional and technical specifications, and to code, test, and train users. Now with a set of innovations in the provision of computing, storage, and networking,

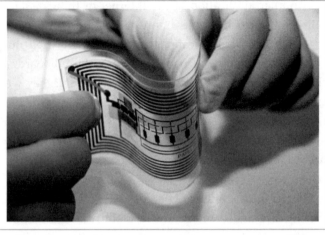

More information stored on each tag could identify when a product is about to pass sell-by date or from where it was sourced

Exhibit 3.13 Advanced RFID tags: More capabilities at less cost.
Source: http://www.wired.com/wiredscience/2010/03/rfid/.[21]

systems can be envisaged, deployed, and enhanced much more quickly. The result of these innovations—cloud computing—will offer new levels of agility to businesses. The ability to change processes across a large-scale multichannel retailer quickly, experiment with new customer experiences and scale up those that work rapidly, and innovate with new business models or partnerships flexibly means that systems deployment will ultimately no longer be a primary constraint on imaginative managers. We expect this to accelerate the pace of change in retail dramatically. The combination of imagination and data-driven insight will become the constrained resource in retail.

What is changing

The development of cloud computing in some ways resembles the evolution of the electricity industry in the 20th century. Just as businesses and farms had to have proprietary generators until they switched to power provided by utilities, so businesses and organizations have had to buy or build proprietary IT systems so they could store data, run programs, and operate their websites. Even if outsourced to an external provider, server and storage systems needed to be provisioned at excess capacity to allow for peak demand. They thus proved costly when measured against peak requirements. But with cloud computing, companies can rent many of the computing resources they need directly from a wide range of service providers over the Internet (Box 3.7).

What it means for retail

Cloud-delivered systems could be the solution to two challenges inherent in retailing: the need to boost operational effectiveness through a better management of IT infrastructure, and the need for new business models to generate sales growth. Three particular features will be relevant to retail:

- **Decapitalization.** By reducing capital requirements for IT investment, cloud computing can transform capital expenditure (and hence fixed depreciation) into variable operating expenses. This creates a more flexible cost structure that varies based on demand. While thoughtful capacity and supply planning are still required, retailers can expand and reduce computing resources as required by shifting application and analytics workloads, and pay according to use.
- **Utilization management.** Seasonality and demand volatility are much feared by retailers, because they increase the complexity of warehouse and inventory management. Today, seasonality relates not only to demand for goods but also to a retailer's IT infrastructure—in terms of servers, network capacity, and storage—and it is managed by the installation of enough capacity to meet projected peak loads (plus a margin for growth) in underlying systems. As a result, the average utilization of data center servers across industries is reported by Gartner to be between 12 and 18 percent of their computing capacity; in our client work, we have frequently found it to be lower in particularly seasonal businesses.[22] Capital productivity and operational efficiency suffer accordingly. Cloud computing enables retailers to address these challenges by allowing for the fast, flexible, on-demand provisioning of additional resources as required. Through the cloud, businesses can

Box 3.7 Cloud computing at a glance

Definition

"Cloud computing" refers to the delivery of software functionality over the Internet from remote data centers. The computing and storage resources in those data centers are shared among a number of the service provider's customers, while the providers' security architecture and procedures keep the customers' data separated and private. Capacity is not fixed but is adjusted as needed to meet varying workloads. (Note that the "cloud" label comes from the cloud shapes used on network diagrams to indicate the public Internet; cloud services are those delivered via the Internet to businesses and consumers.)

Core characteristics

According to the National Institute of Standards and Technology in the United States, cloud computing is shaped by the following characteristics (Exhibit 3.14):

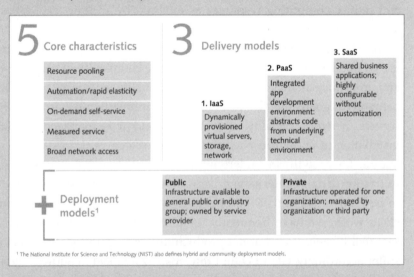

5 Core characteristics

Resource pooling
Automation/rapid elasticity
On-demand self-service
Measured service
Broad network access

3 Delivery models

1. IaaS
Dynamically provisioned virtual servers, storage, network

2. PaaS
Integrated app development environment: abstracts code from underlying technical environment

3. SaaS
Shared business applications; highly configurable without customization

Deployment models¹

Public
Infrastructure available to general public or industry group; owned by service provider

Private
Infrastructure operated for one organization; managed by organization or third party

¹ The National Institute for Science and Technology (NIST) also defines hybrid and community deployment models.

Exhibit 3.14 Overview of core characteristics, service delivery, and deployment models of cloud computing.
Sources: McKinsey Cloud Initiative; NIST.

- **Resource pooling.** The cloud concept is based on the pooling of resources. Computing power is pooled in the cloud so that organizations no longer have to install proprietary systems. They can access computer power far more easily. In effect, they outsource their IT infrastructure and benefit from economies of scale generated by the pool.
- **Automation/rapid elasticity.** The cloud is elastic, enabling it to cater and adapt to the customer's changing requirements. Imagine a customer who needs 100 terabytes of storage today and 500 petabytes of storage tomorrow (i.e. 5,000 times as much) because it has launched a loyalty program that pours data into its system.[21] Through the cloud, storage can be provided without substantial up-front investment.
- **On-demand self-service.** The cloud is a dynamic system that caters to a user's needs for storage capacity, processing power, and software. Users can obtain any type of software, for as long as they need it, without having to pay the cost of installing it.
- **Metered/measured service.** Users do not have to make a capital investment; they are billed for what they use. In accounting terms, the service generates operating expenses and gives companies with more modest IT budgets greater leeway in conducting operations.
- **Broad network access.** Users can access the cloud anywhere, at any time, and through any device. This is what makes the concept so significant. Computing power is no longer restricted to a specific physical location. Rather, it becomes an omnipresent resource.

Service models

The cloud deploys its resources through various service models:

- **IaaS (Infrastructure as a Service).** IaaS is a basic form of cloud computing, in which local IT infrastructure in the shape of servers, networks, and processing units is replaced by remote resources provisioned dynamically to meet workloads. The software platform (i.e. the operating system), data management, and software execution environment are fully determined by the customer, not the service provider.

- **PaaS (Platform as a Service).** PaaS models provide a computing platform and program execution environment. In other words, customers can tap into a cloud service provider's processing power to run their own software. They can take advantage of platform services that allow for greater software development and deployment productivity and avoid buying their own infrastructure and installing and managing the platform layers as well. That enables them to focus fully on writing innovation applications quickly and effectively.
- **SaaS (Software as a Service).** Software as a service is the best-known form of cloud computing. Users can access software on demand through the cloud instead of having to purchase and install it on their own equipment. This means that customers are buying software functionality others write and making it available to their users via the Internet. SaaS eliminates the need for infrastructure, platforms, and software development—though configuration and data management work are still required to prepare a system for rollout to end-users.

Deployment models

The deployment models for the cloud vary between on- and off-premise models and between fully public and restricted models.

Source: Peter Mell and Timothy Grance, "The NIST definition of cloud computing: Recommendations of the National Institute of Standards and Technology," Special Publication 800-145 (NIST, September 2011), http://csrc.nist.gov/publications/nistpubs/800-145/SP800-145.pdf, accessed January 23, 2013.

avoid extreme under- or overutilization and cope with severe demand peaks without having to invest as heavily in excess capacity as they have in the past.

- **Agility and speed.** Cloud-based software delivered as a service can help businesses to be more agile: the software is always up to date, and this mode of delivery allows for a more rapid configuration of functionality and enables users to access applications more easily. Previously, retailers first had to invest large amounts of money and time in installing server infrastructure and storage capacity. Now the cloud allows the adoption of systems that can mirror consumers' changing behavior and use of new technology. Domino's Pizza, for example, uses the cloud to cope with sudden spikes in processing demand. Its pizza is highly popular during halftime at the Super Bowl, but installing excess IT capacity to cope with this peak demand would not be feasible in terms of capital productivity. With cloud computing, Domino's can add IT capacity flexibly, even for just a couple of hours.

Cloud-computing providers can also allow the creation and setup of a new retail business very quickly. An entrepreneur can rent all the software, processing power, and data storage that the new business needs and can have flexible stores, leveraging numerous digital platforms that are operational with just a network connection and a few mobile devices for the staff. Almost all the applications needed for managing a retailer—store POS, online commerce, merchandising, supply chain planning and execution, financial management, and people management—can be acquired "as a service." While these tools may not yet be as feature-rich as their on-premise software counterparts in each domain, they are improving quickly, making cloud delivery an option for both small and medium-sized retailers, as well as larger-scale players. Increasingly, this flexibility extends to set up shop in geographies all around the world as cloud-based software providers improve their multi-language and multi-currency capabilities.

Along with the advantages that cloud computing offers retailers, there are risks. Security is a concern if data moves away from a company. Access to applications and related data becomes highly dependent on the reliability of a network that is outside the control of the chief information officer. And there is the possibility that IT skills, already scarce, could become ever more expensive as demand for them rises.

Nevertheless, cloud computing should be considered a major, industry-changing shift. Its impact will take years to play out as mindsets and capabilities are built, a new ecosystem of providers takes shape, and operating models catch up with the technology's potential.

What's next in the cloud

Albeit at an early stage, certain developments in cloud computing could change the weather for retailers. These include hybrid clouds, new operating models in IT, and "cloud sourcing."

Hybrid clouds combine the public cloud delivery model (off-premises, multi-tenanted) with a private model (on-premises, dedicated) so that workloads can shift from company-owned services or data center facilities to third-party hosts. As the technology and standards for orchestrating these moves mature, retailers will be able to take advantage of truly flexible capacity. While market terms, pricing models, and risk sharing with providers are yet to be defined, this trend should find early adopters in the retail sector as operators seek efficiency while preserving the ability to meet spiky seasonal demands.

Cloud computing and other new delivery processes, such as virtual desktop management and "bring your own device" models (Box 3.8), spark technology teams to rethink their operating processes. Most IT departments have an operating rhythm and a set of management processes built for earlier times, when each new application started with requirements gathering, which drove system architecture, coding, testing, and then acquisition and deployment of hardware. Now the potential of cloud computing to deliver pooled computing, storage, and networking capacity to meet variable workloads is forcing a thorough review of the

Box 3.8 New delivery processes at a glance

Virtual desktop management. Desktop users' files and programs reside on a centralized server, where the IT department can more readily maintain security, deliver updates, and troubleshoot problems. This can reduce costs and time to resolve device-related problems for users.

Bring your own device. The organization allows employees to use their own devices, such as smartphones, tablets, and PCs, so they no longer have to carry as many devices, and user satisfaction with IT support and delivery increases. Web interfaces, cloud delivery, virtual desktop tools, and advances in security software can enable a user's own device to securely access and interact with corporate information.

work and processes required to manage capacity. What used to be a procurement and provisioning process for new hardware, for example, becomes a capacity planning, forecasting, and risk management process for computing and storage. What used to be a process of fixing failed hardware using vendors' field repair teams can become a rapid redeployment of other resources. And what was once a process of disposing of hardware when an application was no longer needed can become a process to reclaim and reuse resources freed up by the decommissioning.

This can lead to substantial increases in the productivity of people and infrastructure. But it demands a mindset in which cloud is the "new normal" delivery model for technology, rather than a complement to traditional models. Given the volume of traditional technology in use and the persistence of traditional mindsets, that shift will take some time to work through.

Eager to help the process along, a "cloud sourcing" industry of service providers is springing up. These services offer capabilities such as Insights as a Service—taking data, mining it for trends, and feeding it back to their clients. Others are quickly rounding up temporary labor to perform important but easily structured tasks such as mystery shopping store visits quickly and cheaply. Services of this kind use Web-based software to recruit shoppers with the right profiles in many cities quickly—and then they capture their reports in cloud-based applications, allowing for instant analysis with no documents to upload or download. This sort of service makes it easier for retailers to vary their cost structures and manage operations with fewer permanent staff. They also, by orchestrating resources outside the company and then integrating the output into the company's processes, further shift the boundaries of what is inside and what is outside the enterprise—continuing and accelerating a decade-long shift toward "unbundling the corporation."[23] Cloud technology will enable retailers to discover and integrate new services from emerging providers around the world more rapidly (and measure the results more accurately), which will drive productivity and innovation.

What it means for consumers

Mobility, measurability, and agility reinforce one another. Mobile devices are able to access cloud-based software through fast networks, for example. Analytics based on measuring consumer trends can deliver ever-more-targeted promotions to mobile devices. And data from smartphones, signaling who is shopping where and how, feed number-crunching experiments that are conducted in the cloud to improve the customer experiment and craft yet more enticing offers.

The potential impact of these technologies on retailers' business is tremendous. But when contemplating the possibilities, it is important to consider the new world from a consumer's perspective too, because a central feature of the digital era is customer empowerment. The tables have turned, and consumers, not retailers, increasingly find themselves in the driver's seat. Consumers have high expectations, and any channel that meets their expectations will reset the bar for what others must deliver. Competition will know no bounds, and customers of the next decade will not be patient with retailers that disappoint. The next chapter explores in more detail how the new technologies have changed consumers' behavior and expectations.

Notes

1. Kelly Wetherille, "Tokyo Girls teams with YouTube," *WWD*, March 4, 2011, Business Insights: Essentials, http://bi.galegroup.com.
2. James Manyika, *et al.*, "Big data: The next frontier of innovation, competition, and productivity," McKinsey Global Institute, May 2011, p. 21, available at http://www.mckinsey.com/insights/mgi/research/technology_and_innovation/big_data_the_next_frontier_for_innovation.
3. Erik Brynjolfsson and Andrew McAfee, "Investing in the IT that makes a competitive difference," *Harvard Business Review* (July 2008).
4. The formula for the number of network connections is $n(n - 1)/2$, where n is the number of network users. Asymptotically, this equals n^2.
5. IDC, "IDC predicts 2012 will be the year of mobile and cloud platform wars as IT vendors vie for leadership while the industry redefines itself," news release, December 1, 2011, http://www.idc.com/getdoc.jsp?containerId=prUS23177411, accessed January 23, 2013.
6. Matt Hamblen, "Smartphones and tablets growth exploding, especially in business, Gartner says," *Computerworld*, November 6, 2012, http://www.computerworld.com/s/article/9233305/Smartphones_and_tablets_growth_exploding_especially_in_business_Gartner_says, accessed January 23, 2013.
7. Sue Stock, "Home Depot used dip to prepare for a boom," *News and Observer (Raleigh, NC)*, June 20, 2010, http://www.newsobserver.com/2010/06/20/540686/home-depot-used-dip-to-prepare.html, accessed January 23, 2013.
8. Arielle Kass, "First Phone permits employees to call Home," *Atlanta Journal-Constitution*, May 31, 2011, http://www.ajc.com/news/business/first-phone-permits-employees-to-call-home/nQts7/, accessed January 23, 2013.
9. Joel Schectman, "Home Depot rolls out new mobile devices for workers," *Wall Street Journal*, June 21, 2012, http://blogs.wsj.com/cio/2012/06/21/home-depot-rolls-out-new-mobile-devices-for-workers/, accessed January 23, 2013.

10. "A look at the Home Depot's 'First Phone,'" *Retail Technology Industry Guide*, March 2011, http://www.retailindustry.com/retail-tech/articles/2011/homedepot-first-phone.html, accessed January 23, 2013.

11. "Droid wars: Smartphones are invading battlefields," *The Economist*, October 8, 2011, http://www.economist.com/node/21531114, accessed January 23, 2013.

12. Elizabeth Woyke, "Raytheon sends Android to battlefield," *Forbes*, October 19, 2009, http://www.forbes.com/2009/10/19/android-google-military-technology-wireless-raytheon.html, accessed January 23, 2013.

13. The QR code is a two-dimensional code, consisting of black square dots on a white background in a square pattern. While conventional bar codes can store approximately 20 digits, the QR code has up to 7,809 characters encoded in one symbol.

14. Brian Barrett, "Augmented reality façade shows buildings real-time deets and tweets," *Gizmodo*, January 12, 2010, http://gizmodo.com/5446228/augmented-reality-facade-shows-buildings-real+time-deets-and-tweets; Sue Bergeron, "Tokyo's N Building: Augmented reality architecture," *VerySpatial.com*, January 12, 2010, http://veryspatial.com/2010/01/tokyos-n-building-augmented-reality-architecture/, accessed January 23, 2013.

15. Website accessed April 23, 2013.

16. Paul Sawers, "Augmented reality: The past, present and future," *The Next Web*, July 3, 2011, http://thenextweb.com/insider/2011/07/03/augmented-reality-the-past-present-and-future/, accessed January 23, 2013.

17. Kevin Bonsor, "How augmented reality works," *HowStuffWorks.com*, February 19, 2001, http://computer.howstuffworks.com/augmented-reality4.htm, accessed January 23, 2013.

18. See James Manyika *et al.*, "Big data: The next frontier of innovation, competition, and productivity," McKinsey Global Institute, May 2011, http://www.mckinsey.com/insights/mgi/research/technology_and_innovation/big_data_the_next_frontier_for_innovation, accessed January 23, 2013; and Brad Brown, Michael Chui, and James Manyika, "The challenge—and opportunity—of 'big data,'" *McKinsey on Business Technology* (Summer 2011), 20–33.

19. Lora Cecere, "Three years of retail RFID pilots," *Forbes*, May 2, 2007, http://www.forbes.com/2007/05/02/amr-rfid-assess-biz-logistics-cx_lc_0502amr.html, accessed January 23, 2013.

20. M. Chui, M. Löffler, and R. Roberts, "The Internet of Things," *McKinsey Quarterly*, no. 2 (2010), pp. 70–79.

21. Website accessed 23 January, 2013.

22. Bill Snyder, "Server virtualization has stalled, despite the hype," *InfoWorld*, December 31, 2010, http://www.infoworld.com/t/server-virtualization/ what-you-missed-server-virtualization-has-stalled-despite-the-hype-901, accessed January 23, 2013.

23. John Hagel III and Marc Singer, "Unbundling the corporation," *Harvard Business Review* (March 1999), http://hbr.org/1999/03/unbundling-the-corporation/ar/1, accessed January 23, 2013.

Chapter 4

Consumer Empowerment

Co-authored with Roger Roberts

Thanks to the retail capabilities made possible by advances in computing, networking, and storage, shopping is more convenient for consumers, who can now browse, select, pay, and take possession, all without entering a store. Retailers have new ways of engaging with their customers, too. But this is only a small aspect of what has changed. Far more significantly, new technologies have put an end to the information asymmetry between retailers and consumers, including—most disruptively—inside the store. In short, customers have been empowered at many retailers' expense.

The catalyst: mobile devices. With or without them, consumers can conduct online price comparisons. But with them, consumers can do this anywhere, at any time. That fact takes customer empowerment into a new dimension.

Retailers have long understood human beings' need for a sense of control and found ways to give their customers a degree of it. One way was by offering self-service, which ended the shopper's dependence on a salesperson. Another is the "no obligation" trial (though the marketer assumes, of course, that most customers will be satisfied with the trial purchase or at least not sufficiently motivated to return it).[1]

In both of these examples, the degree of control that customers have is limited, because the retailer defines its boundaries. But the control offered by the recently emerging innovative technologies is of a different order. This explains their huge uptake by consumers, as well as the shift in the balance of power, now tilting away from retailers and toward consumers.[2]

The consumer decision journey

When consumers buy a product, they embark on a "decision journey" of four stages (Exhibit 4.1). At each stage, marketers can win or lose the customer. The first stage is the initial consideration of a set of brands. The second is evaluation of each brand in the set. The third stage is closure, meaning the selection and purchase of a particular brand. The fourth stage is post-purchase, which is important because a person's experience of the product bought will influence the next decision journey.[3] All journeys progress along the same route. The only thing that varies is the trigger, be it laundry detergent running low or the family car breaking down.

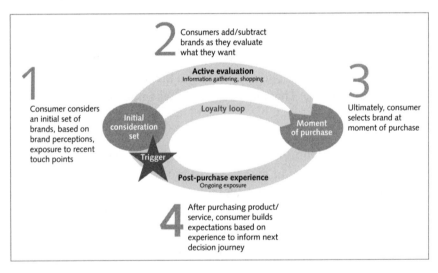

Exhibit 4.1 The consumer decision journey.
Source: David Court *et al.*, "The consumer decision journey," *McKinsey Quarterly*, no. 3 (June 2009), pp. 97–107.

Initial consideration of products and brands is influenced by past perceptions. These are shaped by advertising, experience, and other people. For instance, most individuals can say what sort of car they would buy, whether or not they are about to buy one. Proceeding to the evaluation phase, consumers seek more information about the products under consideration, online and off, steadily refining their choice. At closure, a purchase is made, marking the chosen brand's ability to stay with the customer throughout the decision journey.

The journey does not end there. Consumers' post-purchase experience of the brand will determine whether it will be up for consideration the next time they need the same type of product. Ideally, they will be so satisfied that they will take a shortcut along the "loyalty loop," not even considering other brands. For this reason, many marketers consider the post-purchase stage of the journey the most important.

Technology has not altered the path of this journey. But it has handed power to consumers in a way that dramatically changes their behavior at each stage—and it has done so at retailers' expense.

Customer empowerment tools

Consumers are winning control through the functions on Internet-enabled mobile devices that facilitate product search and research, purchase and payment, and connections to social media. These tools affect the initial consideration and evaluation of a product or service. Consideration is no longer restricted to what one retailer might stock in store, and evaluation criteria are no longer confined to what retailers might say about the product or to the customer's previous purchasing experience. Instead, customers have huge choice and unprecedented transparency as to price and quality.

Take wine. The range on offer in a supermarket or wine merchant can seem overwhelming, yet in-store information is often limited to price and perhaps a recommendation from sales assistants. In all, the experience is not particularly conducive to making an informed purchasing decision. Sometimes, just the look and feel of a bottle will sway the decision.

With an Internet-enabled mobile phone, it is easier to make an informed choice, which need not be limited to the products in the store where the customer happens to be standing. The customer can use a search engine to look for reviews and compare prices at other retailers, or use a mobile app to scan the bar code of a selected wine and show the best offers from online retailers that will deliver. The RedLaser app, for example, enables the user to scan bar codes and instantly receive information on prices elsewhere, along with product reviews.[4] If the customer wants some food to go with the wine, he or she can use Yottamark's Harvestmark Food Traceability app to scan the bar codes of perishable foods and call up information on the provenance of particular items, send feedback, share reviews, and even contact individual farmers or producers. This level of transparency can build customers' trust in their retailers—or destroy it.

From the retailer's point of view, the most unsettling innovation may be Amazon's Price Check app (Exhibit 4.2), which invites customers to scan the bar code of an item in a shop. The app then searches for the same item on Amazon's website—and may respond with an immediate, sometimes cheaper counteroffer for the product.[5] Unsurprisingly, the app has provoked a strong reaction from rival retailers, as it not only enables Amazon to expand sales but also uses customers as agents for the collection of in-store price information. Consumers, however, tend not to complain.

Likewise, PriceGrabber.com has joined forces with several thousand retailers and manufacturers to pool information, enabling consumers to compare the prices of millions of products in 25 categories, including clothing, children's goods, books, magazines, mobile phones and accessories, computers, TVs, furniture, and cameras.[6]

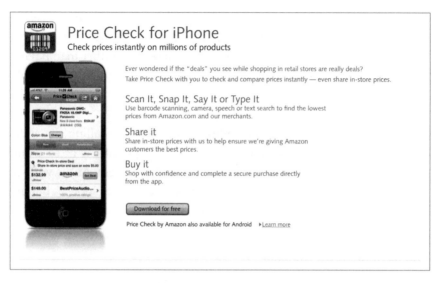

Exhibit 4.2 Amazon's Price Check.
Source: Amazon's website.

Information technology is thus destroying the monopoly retailers once enjoyed over information about products and prices. In so doing, it is transferring some control over prices to consumers, who can give their business to whichever retailer offers the best deal. Already in 2010, 75 percent of respondents to the McKinsey European iConsumer retail survey said they had researched and purchased goods online during a three-month period.[7] In addition, 44 percent of mobile-phone owners said they had used a mobile device inside a store for research purposes: 43 percent to visit the store's own website while in the store, 40 percent to view a competitor's site, and 38 percent to use price comparison tools.[8]

Mobile purchase and payment

With a mobile device, consumers can select, purchase, and pay for products at any time, anywhere, and arrange for goods to be delivered to their homes. (The payment functionality is enabled by a technology known as near-field communication, or NFC.) Shopping is no longer limited by store opening hours or even access to a PC. Even when consumers go shopping in-store, mobile devices can simplify processes. An entire basket of items can be scanned in one go, and receipts can be sent directly to a handheld device, making them easier to manage. And rather than paying for goods on the spot, customers can have bills added to, say, a monthly phone invoice.

Furnished with so much flexibility, consumers are calling the shots about how, when, and where they shop. Their expectations of ease and convenience are rising—and the retailer must satisfy them. As we will see later in this chapter, retailers are beginning to try many responses but are still in the experimental stage with these.

Connections to social media

Hundreds of millions of people use social media. Even so, the exact meaning and relevance of social media baffle many individuals, who do not belong to the generation of "digital natives"—a term coined by the American writer Marc Prensky to describe a person born during or after the general inception of digital technologies.[9] For retailers, however, an understanding of how these tools influence and empower consumers is crucial.

The term *social media* refers to any online channel that is available to an extended audience, builds upon and relates to other content, and enables users to become producers of the content.[10] It includes networking sites such as Facebook, along with microblogs, media- and file-sharing sites, gaming sites, and other applications for creating and sharing content (Exhibit 4.3).

The sector has grown explosively (Exhibit 4.4). In 2011, 81 percent of Internet users participated in social media, up from 50 percent in 2003, and consumers are spending an ever-greater proportion of their time on social networks.[11] A recent survey of ten global markets by NM Incite, a social-media intelligence company, revealed that social networks and blogs were the top online destinations in each market, used by more than

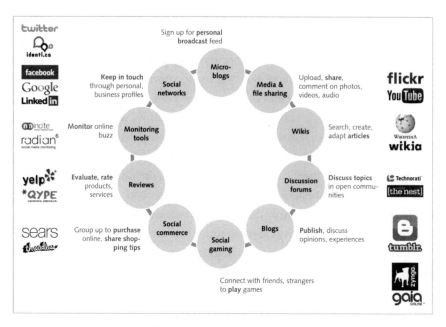

Exhibit 4.3 Social-media formats.
Source: McKinsey.

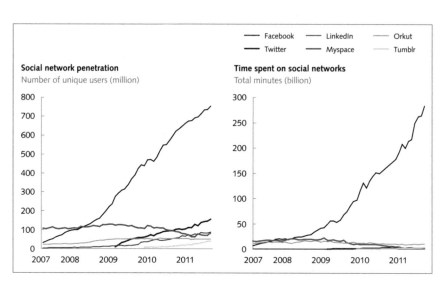

Exhibit 4.4 Skyrocketing global growth in social network.
Source: ComScore, McKinsey.

three-quarters of active Internet users.[12] Leading platforms such as Facebook and Twitter have amassed hundreds of millions of active users, all of whom are effectively broadcasters and engaging with their online community in real time.[13] Indeed, the NM Incite survey found that 60 percent (and rising) of active social-network users post their own product and service reviews, while more than 50 percent follow a brand.[14] About 70 percent of active social networkers say they read the reviews.[15]

Again, the key implication for retailers is consumer empowerment. The sentiment expressed by even a single person about a brand or company can be quickly amplified on a massive scale, while social media bestow a level of credibility on the opinions of users that can be far greater than that of a company or brand. Together, amplification and credibility can have a huge impact on brand perception, customer loyalty, sales, and even share price.

Amplification

A US transportation company learned the power of social media after an item it was transporting got damaged by rough handling. The owner tried for a year to get compensation and eventually posted a video about the incident on YouTube. Within days, the video received more than 100,000 hits, and within 18 months, 10 million. The footage still triggers negative comments about the company.

By contrast, UK supermarket chain Sainsbury's created a positive social buzz with its response to a letter from a three-year-old girl who questioned the branding of its Tiger Bread, so called because of the stripes on the crust. She wrote that the loaf reminded her more of a giraffe, and that it should be renamed. Sainsbury's customer service team replied, calling her idea "brilliant," and the girl's mother wrote about the exchange on her blog. Seven months later, the exchange with the retailer became hugely popular on social-media sites. A single post on Facebook prompted more than 150,000 "likes" and 48,000 "shares," which were followed by

Exhibit 4.5 Sainsbury's now-famous Giraffe Bread.
Source: Sainsbury's website, http://j-sainsbury.co.uk/media/443631/
giraffebread.jpg.

thousands of tweets via Twitter, hundreds of blog posts, and widespread media coverage.[16] Sainsbury's quickly responded by changing the product's name to Giraffe Bread (Exhibit 4.5).

The example illustrates another point. Just as consumer sentiment can be magnified by social media, so can the reaction to it of a company or brand. Sainsbury's response drew a massive amount of positive attention in social and traditional media.[17] By contrast, when a food manufacturer was targeted by a Greenpeace video calling attention to what the organization claimed was the company's environmentally damaging use of palm oil, its reaction dug it deeper into a hole. It sought to prevent the video being shown, on the grounds of trademark violations, to which Greenpeace responded by encouraging people to comment on the manufacturer's Facebook page. The company tried to limit the damage to its reputation by deleting selected comments, which only drew further attention to the video, until more than a million people had watched it on YouTube. Eventually, the company was pressured into stating that it would work with a nonprofit environmental organization to pursue environmentally sustainable goals.

Credibility

Whom would you trust most to give an honest opinion about a product: the retailer, the manufacturer, or friends and all those online consumers who have actually purchased the item and not profited from its sale? It is a question that exercises the minds of many of today's retailers. Already, the majority of consumers say they pay attention to recommendations made by other users on a retailer's website (Exhibit 4.6). In addition, social-media users are those most likely to be influenced by other online consumers.[18] Just how credible the opinions of online consumers ultimately become among so much online activity remains to be seen. But their potential to influence cannot be ignored, and it explains the growing social-media activity of many retailers.

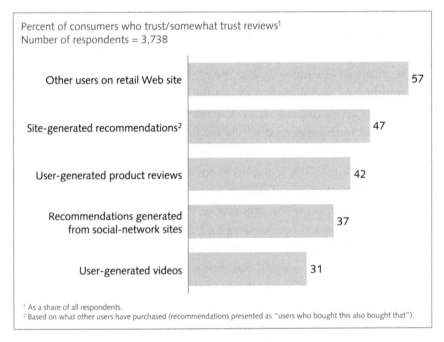

Percent of consumers who trust/somewhat trust reviews[1]
Number of respondents = 3,738

Other users on retail Web site — 57
Site-generated recommendations[2] — 47
User-generated product reviews — 42
Recommendations generated from social-network sites — 37
User-generated videos — 31

[1] As a share of all respondents.
[2] Based on what other users have purchased (recommendations presented as "users who bought this also bought that").

Exhibit 4.6 Social network recommendations that consumers trust.
Source: McKinsey iConsumer retail survey (2011).

Retailers' response to consumers' changing behavior

Retailers are responding to their newly empowered customers by experimenting. Some are responding to price transparency by making their products harder to compare, perhaps by adding private labels, bundling items, or changing product sizes. Many try to satisfy customers' wish for convenience—for example by using technology to make in-store shopping and the checkout process a good deal easier for their customers. Nordstrom, the US clothing chain, offers a mobile app that enables the user not only to browse, read customer reviews, and interact with friends but also to check product availability at nearby stores. Customers no longer have to risk going to a shop only to find that what they want is not in stock. Still other retailers are harnessing the reach and credibility of social media to help customers evaluate products. Other ideas include price matching, location signaling, social-media engagement, and more. Let's take a closer look at some of the innovations retailers have tried as they seek ways to address the three areas of customer empowerment—transparency, convenience, and social media.

Transparency

In a world where pricing is transparent, some retailers are embracing the transparency by using technology to guarantee to match the lowest price offered elsewhere. UK retailer Sainsbury's launched a scheme in 2011 called the Sainsbury's Brand Match.[19] When a customer spends £20 or more, has bought at least one branded product, and could have purchased the same item for less at rivals Asda or Tesco on the same day, Sainsbury's offers the customer a coupon to make up the difference.[20] The coupon is valid at Sainsbury's for up to two weeks.

How does it work? Sainsbury's uses a technique known as data scraping, which involves collecting data published on other organizations' websites and using the data to populate Sainsbury's own price comparison database. Every night at midnight, Sainsbury's scrapes the (over

20,000) online prices published by its main competitors, Tesco and Asda. When a customer goes through a Sainsbury's checkout, the price for each item is compared against the competing prices in the database. If Sainsbury's was more expensive, the register automatically and instantaneously generates a coupon to make up the difference. If Sainsbury's was cheaper, the customer's receipt shows by how much. If customers want, they can go online and see a detailed item-by-item comparison of their basket and a running total of how much they've saved at Sainsbury's over the previous eight weeks.

Another approach to transparency is to heighten and then satisfy consumers' hunger for a bargain. Retailers are using personal-location signaling to entice people into their stores. The signaling detects when an individual who has subscribed to the retailers' program is close to a location or enters a geo-fence (a real-world geographic area marked by a virtual perimeter defined, for instance, by signals of telegraph poles). When this occurs, the retailer sends the person's mobile device a message with promotions, advertisements, or vouchers. There is evidence suggesting that at least some consumers welcome being targeted in this way. In a survey, 65 percent of those who used location apps said they did so to get promotions, and 78 percent said they considered actually using the promotions (Exhibit 4.7).

Simply entering a shop can encourage impulse buying, of course. Well-known retailers such as Levi's, Target, Macy's, and Toys "R" Us therefore see potential in signing up to make offers on the Shopkick app. This mobile app rewards consumers with items such as a free cappuccino just for walking into participating stores. Launched in August 2011, Shopkick had one million users after six months and two million after ten months (Exhibit 4.8).

Convenience

Retailers have developed various apps that seek to make shopping at their stores more convenient. Wal-Mart's multifunctional iPhone/iPad app, for

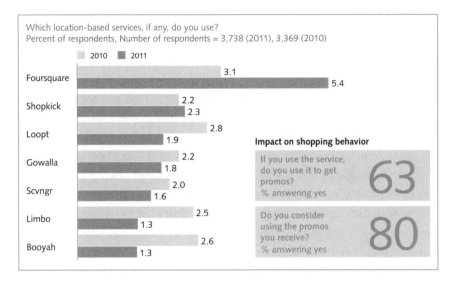

Which location-based services, if any, do you use?
Percent of respondents, Number of respondents = 3,738 (2011), 3,369 (2010)

2010 ■ 2011

Service	2010	2011
Foursquare	3.1	5.4
Shopkick	2.2	2.3
Loopt	2.8	1.9
Gowalla	2.2	1.8
Scvngr	2.0	1.6
Limbo	2.5	1.3
Booyah	2.6	1.3

Impact on shopping behavior

If you use the service, do you use it to get promos? % answering yes **63**

Do you consider using the promos you receive? % answering yes **80**

Exhibit 4.7 Localization services can be a powerful tool to leverage online.
Source: McKinsey iConsumer retail survey (2011).

Exhibit 4.8 Rewarded by the Shopkick app.
Source: Shopkick's website, http://www.shopkick.com.

example, has a shopping list that users can edit by typing, scanning bar codes, or using Apple's Siri voice command system. In helping consumers in this way, Wal-Mart has what many loyalty card programs do not: data on what shoppers are considering buying, rather than actually buying. Wal-Mart can then make recommendations based on the shopping list. The shopping list is automatically matched with vouchers from Coupons. com, one of the largest independent voucher search engines. The app also checks product availability in nearby stores and the location of products in individual stores, and it has budget-keeping functionality to help customers keep track of their spending. It seamlessly combines online and offline activities, transferring aspects of the shopping experience typically associated with e-commerce into the store.[21] The app has important benefits for Wal-Mart, helping it to reduce sales staff and collect more information about its customers' shopping behavior, but in the process, the customer's shopping experience is significantly improved.

Dutch retailer Ahold also is using consumers' mobile devices to increase its own productivity and to offer its customers a more convenient, quicker service (Exhibit 4.9). Ahold's app ScanIt! Mobile allows

Exhibit 4.9 Self-scanning at Ahold.
Source: Ann Zimmerman, "Check out the future of shopping," *Wall Street Journal*,
May 18, 2011, http://online.wsj.com/article/
SB10001424052748703421204576329253050637400.html.

Exhibit 4.10 Emart smart cart in Korea.
Source: Economic Review, http://www.econovill.com/archives/41547.

customers to scan the products they buy, speeding up the checkout process as the information is automatically transferred to the till. For customers without a smartphone, Ahold provides its own handheld device.

In a similar fashion, Korean retailer Emart, together with SK Telecom, has explored using a smart shopping cart that provides consumers with information on product location, promotions, and real-time updates on consumers' accumulated membership points as they load their carts (Exhibit 4.10). Consumers who use such a cart would be able to view and save shopping information using their smartphone, which would be synchronized with the smart-cart device at their next purchase.

Tesco has even experimented to help consumers shop while they wait for a train. In so doing, the retailer has embraced mobile as a sales channel but combined it with the highest levels of customer convenience. Its virtual grocery store—located in Korea—displays photos of the store shelves in subway stations (Exhibit 4.11). While waiting for the train, people can use their smartphone cameras to capture QR codes of the items

Exhibit 4.11 Tesco's virtual subway store in Korea.
Source: Yonhap news.

displayed and add them to a virtual shopping cart. Payment also is made on the smartphone, and the purchased goods can be delivered conveniently to the consumer's front door.

Social media

While some retailers are using location-based marketing to lure customers into stores, others are building store traffic and sales by engaging with consumers on social media. Conceding that social media make family and friends more influential brand promoters than they are, forward-thinking retailers are looking for ways to translate seemingly independent social-networking activities into an appeal to buy. Clothes retailer C&A has equipped garment hangers in its outlets in Brazil with digital counters that show how many times a particular item has been "liked" on Facebook. Presumably, consumers will be more amenable to buying a well-liked item. In that sense, retailers are inducing consumers to wield some of their power to help the stores.

Other, less subtle efforts couple the harnessing of social media with an appeal to consumers' price consciousness. The store manager of a global retailer, in order to promote the opening of a new store, uploaded images of different showrooms at the store to his personal Facebook photo album and made them accessible to the public. Visitors to the pages were encouraged to tag products; the first person to do so would get that item for free. The campaign spread on Facebook like wildfire as the pictures of showrooms appeared on the taggers' profile pages.

In another promotion revealing what social-network participants are willing to do for retailers, Burger King in January 2009 introduced the Whopper Sacrifice, a Facebook app that offered a free Whopper hamburger to anyone who deleted ten people from his or her list of Facebook friends. Ostensibly, Burger King was asking consumers to value a hamburger more highly than a friend. Once the friends had been deleted, a message was posted on the Facebook user's activity feed, saying something along the lines of, "Nicolas sacrificed Jane Jackson for a free Whopper." As this feed was visible in Facebook, the app created publicity with every deletion—of which there were 200,000 in the first week. Although Facebook quickly disabled the Whopper Sacrifice app, citing privacy concerns, the campaign won numerous marketing prizes.[22]

As clever as many of these ideas may be, all of them are merely experiments; no one suggests they are the end game. What that will be remains unclear. What *is* clear is that the technologies that empower customers and enable retailers in ways hitherto unimaginable are bringing about three major paradigm shifts that will force traditional retailers to adapt their business models. Long-held beliefs about retail are no longer sustainable.

Notes

1. In the mail-order business, return rates have traditionally run at 25 to 30 percent or even more, and Internet retailers report similar figures. The price of reverse logistics, fragmented old stock, and stock loss (for, inevitably, some returns are not suitable for resale) is notionally borne by retailers, but their

pricing structure reflects the cost of this justified sense of control for all customers.

2. In 2011, 36 percent of US consumers surveyed said they had used or would consider using their mobile phones to make a purchase. Moreover, out of the 74.8 percent of US consumers who did research for purchases, 22.8 percent conducted this research on a mobile device. McKinsey & Company, iConsumer research 2011.

3. David Court *et al.*, "The consumer decision journey," *McKinsey Quarterly* (June 2009), pp. 97–107; available at https://www.mckinseyquarterly.com/The_consumer_decision_journey_2373.

4. RedLaser home page, http://redlaser.com, accessed January 23, 2013.

5. Nigam Arora, "Amazon commits rare strategic blunder using brilliant tactic," *Forbes*, December 12, 2011, http://www.forbes.com/sites/greatspeculations/2011/12/12/amazon-commits-rare-strategic-blunder-using-brilliant-tactic/, accessed January 23, 2013; and Erik Kain, "Amazon Price Check may be evil but it's the future," *Forbes*, December 14, 2011, http://www.forbes.com/sites/erikkain/2011/12/14/amazon-price-check-may-be-evil-but-its-the-future/, accessed January 23, 2013.

6. PriceGrabber.com home page, http://pricegrabber.com, accessed January 23, 2013.

7. The iConsumer survey is a proprietary longitudinal customer survey conducted annually by McKinsey. It is aimed at understanding changing consumer behavior across digital experiences, including watching video, listening to music, gaming, using social networks, communicating on the go, buying online, and reading or browsing. The iConsumer Panel covers 20,000 respondents across 12 countries. McKinsey & Company, iConsumer research 2010.

8. Evan Duncan and Kevin Roche, "The next stage: Six ways the digital consumer is changing," paper presented at Chief Marketing and Sales Officer Forum, May 2012, available at http://cmsoforum.mckinsey.com/article/the-next-stage-six-ways-the-digital-consumer-is-changing, accessed January 23, 2013.

9. Marc Prensky, "Digital natives, digital immigrants," *On the Horizon* (MCB University Press) 9, no. 5 (October 2001).

10. Frank Mattern *et al.* "Turn buzz into gold," McKinsey & Company, 2012.

11. Juan Bertiche *et al.* "Creating a social-media strategy," *McKinsey Knowledge Bulletin* (October 2011), p. 1.

12. NM Incite is a joint venture by McKinsey & Company and Nielsen providing social media intelligence. For more information, see http://www.nmincite.com,

accessed January 23, 2013. Countries surveyed included Australia, Brazil, France, Germany, Italy, Japan, Spain, Switzerland, the United States, and the United Kingdom. See Nielsen and NM Incite, "State of the media: The social media report," Q3 2011, http://blog.nielsen.com/nielsenwire/social/, accessed January 23, 2013.

13. Twitter, "One hundred million voices," *Twitter Blog*, September 8, 2011, http://blog.twitter.com/2011/09/one-hundred-million-voices.html, accessed January 23, 2013; Facebook, "Key facts," Facebook Newsroom, http://newsroom.fb.com/content/default.aspx?NewsAreaId=22, accessed January 23, 2013.

14. See Nielsen and NM Incite, "State of the media: The social media report," Q3 2011, available at http://blog.nielsen.com/nielsenwire/social/, accessed January 23, 2013.

15. Bertiche *et al.*, "Creating a social-media strategy," *McKinsey Knowledge Bulletin* (October 2011), p. 1.

16. J Sainsbury PLC, "Why we're renaming Tiger Bread to Giraffe Bread," J Sainsbury plc media page, January 31, 2012, http://j-sainsbury.co.uk/giraffebread, accessed January 23, 2013.

17. Natalie Brandweiner, "CRM: What can Sainsbury's Tiger Bread tale teach us?" *MyCustomer.com*, February 8, 2012, http://www.mycustomer.com/topic/crm-what-can-sainsbury-s-tiger-bread-tale-teach-us/136844, accessed January 23, 2013.

18. According to McKinsey's iConsumer report 2010, 66 to 70 percent of Facebook and/or Twitter users trust recommendations of other online users.

19. "Sainsbury's follows rivals in price promotions," *BBC News*, October 9, 2011, http://www.bbc.co.uk/news/business-15232931, accessed January 23, 2013.

20. Sainsbury's, "Sainsbury's Brand Match," http://www.sainsburys-live-well-for-less.co.uk/brand-match/, accessed January 23, 2013.

21. Jack Neff, "Walmart rolls out new iPad, updated iPhone apps for relationship program," *Advertising Age*, November 9, 2011, http://adage.com/article/digital/walmart-rolls-ipad-updated-iphone-apps-relationship-program/230896/, accessed January 23, 2013.

22. Duncan Macleod, "Burger King Whopper Sacrifice," *The Inspiration Room*, June 22, 2009, http://theinspirationroom.com/daily/2009/burger-king-whopper-sacrifice/, accessed January 23, 2013.

Chapter 5

Toward A New Retailing Paradigm

Co-authored with Nina Gillmann

Technology is severing retail from its past. It is transforming both the way companies in the retail value chain operate and the way they relate to one another and to consumers.

Three important shifts are taking place. First, the importance of the physical store is diminishing as more customers research and buy online. Second, the retail business system no longer has clear boundaries. This means newcomers can contest the territory once dominated by traditional, store-based retailers, such that anyone who can convene customer traffic can, in principle, become a retailer today. Third, big data and the technological improvements described in Chapter 3 have the potential to drive retailers' efficiency and their ability to serve their customers well to new heights. It is a step change in what we call information productivity.

The first two shifts reflect how technology, which once helped consolidate the retailer's position as the intermediary between supplier and consumer, has shifted the entire basis of competition. The retailing tasks of preselection, aggregation, sales advice, and the physical movement of stock are no longer the value-creating preserve of traditional retailers. This poses huge challenges to those whose thinking and operations are still anchored in the old-world model. The third shift reflects the huge opportunities that technology can deliver in retailing's digital era—to old and new participants alike.

The changing role of the physical store

Until now, the physical store has been a self-evident necessity for the retailer and consumer. With the exception of mail-order catalogs, the store was the only place consumers could buy products, or indeed get much information about what was available to purchase. In other words, it was the only platform for the four retailing tasks, so retailers effectively owned the customers in their catchment areas.

Technology has changed all this, undermining the store's value proposition. Online retailers can aggregate demand on a far greater scale, as their "catchment area" knows no bounds.[1] The store's range of goods—the preselection—may now disappoint, given the limitless variety that online retailers collectively select for their customers. And while stores can still dispense valuable sales advice, other channels, particularly social media, are powerful in this respect, too.

Store sales have already suffered as a result. Exhibit 5.1 shows the extent to which different categories of goods and services are already researched and purchased online, and the speed at which this landscape is changing. Many low-involvement categories, such as DVDs, have already "gone to digital," meaning that more than half of those who recently bought the product either researched the product online or bought it online (or both), according to McKinsey research. More will follow.

What does this paradigm shift mean for stores of the future? The answer lies in reviewing the reasons that have traditionally prompted consumers to visit stores, then considering which ones will still stand up to digital competition. The exercise reveals that the physical store still has value, but as we will see in Chapter 6 the business model a store-based retailer chooses will have to make very clear to consumers just exactly what that value is. Customers will still enter a store rather than shop online for one or more of six reasons (Exhibit 5.2).

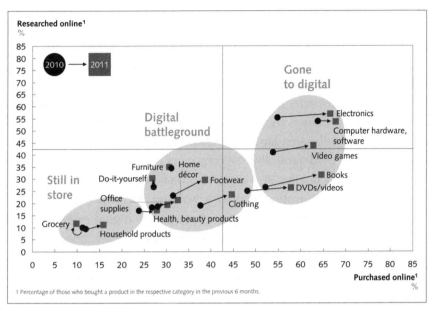

Exhibit 5.1 Trend toward online research and purchase.
Source: McKinsey iConsumer retail survey (2010-11), United States.

Exhibit 5.2 Six reasons to enter a store.
Source: McKinsey.

Instant gratification

Online channels may offer unlimited choice and convenience, but when it comes to instant gratification only in a physical store can consumers get what they need right now. For certain products and in certain circumstances, instant ownership is the key. Consumers often need to buy food for a meal immediately, purchase a forgotten item, or replace something without delay—a broken laptop power cord, perhaps. Stores today often fulfill this need by default. But the concept is more consciously exploited by US electronics retailer Best Buy, which has responded to consumers' need for instant gratification by placing vending machines at airports. The machines carry phone and computer accessories, digital cameras, flash drives, MP3 players, headphones, gaming devices, travel adapters, and other items likely to appeal to customers on the go.[2] Similarly, Get & Go operates unstaffed "stores" with a series of automated machines that offer merchandise and services such as ATM machines, DVD rental, coin counting, coupons, gift cards, ice, cold drinks, snacks, and sandwiches.

Stores can also fulfill urgent demand for more desire-based products—the proof being in the long lines of people who camp out overnight in front of stores to be one of the first to buy the latest iPad, Nike trainers, or *Harry Potter* book.

Once customers are in the store, physical retailers have an advantage over online competitors in their capacity to encourage impulse buying. Impulse buying can happen in both channels. But only in physical stores can consumers see, touch, and test products. Parents know only too well how children clamor for sweets and chocolate displayed at the supermarket checkout—an important source of sales for such food categories. And few customers of any age get as far as the checkout without having responded to a special offer or a well-merchandised new product. The physical display of products remains instrumental in creating the impulse for consumption, so bricks-and-mortar retailers can capitalize on their traditional capabilities by improving window displays, storefronts, product displays, and promotional activities.

Experience products and brands

Consumers may no longer need to enter a store to research and purchase products, but shopping has long been more than a transaction. It is a sensory experience, and people will continue to be attracted to stores to see and touch products and, in some categories, to experience a brand's lifestyle and values.

McKinsey's iConsumer 2010 survey asked people who bought online after visiting a store why they visited a store beforehand. The main reasons were that they either "wanted to touch, feel, test the item" or went to the store to "compare products."[3] So while digital channels may be able to satisfy customers' need for information about products, only a store can satisfy their desire for sensory input. Pure online retailers sometimes offer a free-returns service, recognizing that many customers are reluctant to buy products they cannot first see or try on. But buyers may still find the returns process inconvenient, while the online retailer incurs extra shipping and processing costs.

Unfortunately for stores, it is not always easy to convert this clear physical advantage into sales. Many consumers, having seen what they want in a store, go online to make their purchases more cheaply. Physical retailers thus risk becoming a showroom for their online rivals, with severe financial consequences. Revenues will inevitably fall as customers migrate online, but the cost of operating and maintaining stores remains high.

Stores can take some measures to prevent this "showrooming," as discussed in Chapter 6. The example set by international restaurant and grocery chain Eataly shows how a powerful experience can be used to support sales. Each of its restaurants sits next to a "market area"— a grocery store that sells the fresh ingredients and other high-quality Italian produce that diners have just enjoyed (Exhibit 5.3).[4] What better time to buy?

Exhibit 5.3 Eataly in New York City.
Source: Eataly's website, http://www.eataly.com.

Convenience

Conventional wisdom suggests that buying online wins hands down when it comes to convenience. But conventional wisdom is wrong if shops are located close enough to the places where people live or work. Convenience has increasing value. A recent global study showed that 56 percent of consumers preferred to shop in a local store.[5] And in a study carried out in Germany, young consumers were shortening their travel time to stores. In 2006, almost 50 percent of young consumers drove less than five minutes to do their main shopping, and by 2011, that figure was 55 percent (Exhibit 5.4). Older people have always preferred the convenience of local shops.[6]

In response, retailers are developing new, smaller formats in urban and suburban locations to satisfy local demand. They usually focus on food and other basic products. The German food retailer Rewe, for example, launched Rewe City in 2009, converting 170 of its stores into the convenience format. The stores, which range in area from 500 to 1,000 square meters, offer a limited assortment of 8,000 products, with the focus on fresh, organic, and local produce. Importantly, the stores stay open until

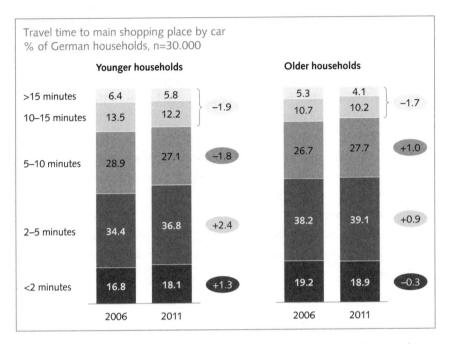

Exhibit 5.4 Seeking convenience: Younger consumers increasingly shop nearby.
Source: GfK ConsumerScan.

10 p.m. or even midnight in some locations, in a country where many stores shut at 8 p.m. Yet it is not only food that people want to buy locally. The French hardware and furniture store But, for instance, has launched a city-center format that, at 800 to 1,000 square meters, is a third of the size of the original format. The store meets consumers' wishes for convenience and for the ability to see and try out items of furniture. Still more convenient, particularly for those at work all day, is But's offer of express home delivery, free of charge, between 8 and 11 p.m.

Some click-and-collect formats cater to the demand for convenience. French grocery retailer Leclerc operates 271 drive-through express stores, or "drives," as they are known in France. Customers can order online and then either pick up their purchase inside the store or have it brought to their cars in areas close to the store. They can also use on-site electronic ordering machines and get their purchases delivered to their cars in less than 15 minutes. Auchan operates a similar click-and-collect format through its Chronodrive and Auchan Drive stores. According to a recent survey, 80 percent of those who visit drives in France do so to gain time, while 64 percent say they do so for the convenience of not having to carry heavy bags.[7] Noticeably, 80 percent of them live less than 10 minutes from the drive.

A word of warning: in the past, consumers have found it convenient to visit large stores, be they hypermarkets, department stores, or big-box specialists, where everything they might need is under one roof. This definition of convenience was the *raison d'être* of the first department stores. In the digital era, however, physical stores modeled on this definition may struggle to remain competitive. Chapter 6 discusses this in greater detail.

Entertainment and social interaction

People go shopping not just because they need something but also for social contact. Friends and family might shop together for fun; older people who lead isolated lives might strike up relationships with staff at the local grocery and socialize with neighbors they bump into.

The role that shopping plays as a source of entertainment and an occasion for socializing explains the success of developments such as Bluewater, a retail and leisure complex in Kent, in the United Kingdom. Beautifully landscaped, Bluewater's attractions succeed in keeping customers on site for an average of three hours. The importance of this role in attracting shoppers also explains how Warnaco, a fashion company in New York City that manufactures and sells underwear and lingerie, managed to reverse declining lingerie sales when it created spaces in its stores for groups of friends to try on products together.[8]

Stores of the future may have to work harder to exploit the social dimension of shopping, given that social interaction is increasingly sought

Exhibit 5.5 Pull & Bear 2.0.
Source: Pull & Bear.

within online social networks. Some retailers are exploring how they can meld the in-store shopping experience with online social interaction—a phenomenon known as "social retailing" in an offline context, and "social commerce" in an online one. Sportswear manufacturer Adidas, for example, has a so-called Social Mirror in the changing rooms of some of its NEO-branded stores. It is a full-size, flat screen that serves as both a mirror and a camera that can take pictures to share instantly on social platforms as a way to seek opinions from friends.[9] Similarly, in 2011, Spain's Inditex, owner of the Pull & Bear clothing brand, which targets young consumers, opened its first interactive store. Named Pull & Bear 2.0, the store boasts the latest in-store technology. Besides fitting rooms where customers can take pictures and post them on Facebook, it has a lounge area with sofas and iMacs that customers can use to access the brand's website and blog, as well as their own social-media accounts (Exhibit 5.5).

Exhibit 5.6 Waiting lines in front of New York Apple store, Grand Central Station. *Source:* Business Insider.

Despite the encroachment of the online world, entertainment and interaction in the real world still have high value. The opening of Apple's Grand Central Station store in New York in December 2011 drew huge crowds, even though there was no new-product launch (Exhibit 5.6). Visitors were eager to admire the way the store had been integrated into the old station's architecture, but social interaction played a role, too. Visitors to the store commented on how they enjoyed being with fellow enthusiasts. And in all Apple stores, customers say they appreciate interacting with the members of the technical support staff, who are always eager to help out. As Apple proclaims, it is the experience, not the product, that pulls customers into stores.[10]

Box 5.1 gives more examples of the ways in which retailers have adapted to meet the needs of today's consumers for entertainment and social interaction.

Box 5.1 Entertaining, sociable retail environments: BOXPARK and Tsutaya

It was with an explicit view to providing social interaction that BOXPARK set up shop in Shoreditch, a trendy part of London. As the name suggests, it is an assembly of containers that have been stripped and refitted to create low-cost, low-risk "box shops" (Exhibit 5.7). The shops sell international fashion, smaller brands, and an array of arts and lifestyle products. Other containers house cafés and galleries. The low-cost/low-risk ethos is deliberate to create a striking product mix. But BOXPARK also aspires to become an integral part of the local community, where retailers can strike up relationships with their customers, and customers enjoy socializing.

An almost mainstream approach to recognizing the importance of socializing while shopping has become the addition of an in-store lounge area or even a café to the retailer's product offering. But the latest generation of in-store lounges bears little resemblance to earlier

Exhibit 5.7 BOXPARK in Shoreditch, London.
Source: Boxpark.

incarnations. Retailers that do it well have managed to interpret the in-store lounge and social interaction as an integral part of the brand.

In December 2011, Tsutaya Books opened a new flagship bookstore in Tokyo that it branded as "a creative third place between home and work" (Exhibit 5.8). The bookstore features a low-lit café-lounge with plush leather seats, to which it invites anyone to come to read, relax, meet friends, or work from his or her laptop.

Exhibit 5.8 Tsutaya bookstore in Tokyo: A place between home and work.
Source: Tsutaya.

Find a solution

Millions of consumers go online to search out product information, be it an answer to which product best suits their needs, how to set up a computer, or how to fix a broken household device. But searching for exactly the right information can be difficult and time-consuming, and not everyone will be confident that he or she has hit upon the right solution online.

Hence, customers will continue to enter the physical store if they believe they can reasonably expect to solve a problem more easily or more expertly with the help of a sales assistant. They might want to get help choosing a new bike, a lamp, or piece of furniture that will look fantastic at home, or the right makeup for a certain type of skin. Perhaps they want advice about building something at home—a fishpond or a new heating installation. Others may seek advice on whether a gadget can be mended or needs replacing.

The opportunity to learn may be an enticing part of the value proposition. Do-it-yourself (DIY) specialist Home Depot not only gives advice on the best tool for the job, it also runs workshops in stores, where customers can find out how to do various home improvements and learn about energy-efficient lighting. Similarly, Italy's Eataly, mentioned earlier, runs cookery and Italian-language classes.

Since price sensitivity for services is low, margins can be high—a particularly attractive proposition in categories with low margins on standard products. Moreover, the offer of customer solutions that depend on or are improved by physical interaction is a selling proposition that online retailers cannot match.

Buy it more cheaply

Some physical retailers can beat online retailers on price because they have learned how to operate physical stores at very low cost by offering a narrow range of goods with very little elaboration or expense in presentation. These so-called hard discounters, including Aldi and Lidl, are popular with customers who enjoy the low prices resulting when retailers combine the scale advantages of very large purchase quantities with the operating efficiency of a simple environment replicated across their network of stores, around which they can organize their warehousing and distribution functions.

Retailers that operate physical stores may also be able to compete on price on certain items because, unlike their online rivals, they do not incur delivery costs. Online retailers enjoy the cost advantages of centralized storage and digital presentation. But the cost of the "last mile"—from the distribution center to the customer's doorstep—can be expensive, not least because of rising consumer expectations, including the wish for same-day delivery. Physical stores, in contrast, get customers to provide last-mile delivery services themselves by coming into the store and taking their purchases home with them. Online retailers can, of course, charge for delivery, but that makes their products more expensive, whether the price difference comes in the form of a direct delivery cost or the cost built into the product price and margin on products delivered "free."

Store operators that also operate a click-and-collect option may be able to offer better prices still, as some multichannel retailers offer lower prices online than in-store. Add to that the convenience of shopping online and (almost) instant gratification, and you have a considerable amount of customer value tied up in the store. And in some cases, for instance in consumer electronics, once customers have ordered and purchased online and are in the store to collect, some will buy more.

New contenders

The changing role of the store is a symptom of a larger change wrought by technology: the erosion of boundaries across the entire business system. Anyone who can convene traffic can use technology to act as a retailer, aggregating consumer demand. Manufacturers can establish direct sales channels to their customers, logistics operators can branch out into selling products, and completely new players can offer a broad assortment of products and services through a network of suppliers, creating potentially huge new markets. The trading of secondhand clothes, once highly fragmented and restricted to local stores and flea markets, is now a global market, owing to the likes of eBay, which has become one of the largest online marketplaces in the world. But even though online channels are blurring the conventional boundaries of retail, not all players have the same source of competitive advantage, or indeed will be equally competitive in the digital era, as we shall see in Chapter 6. Here we describe just some of the new contenders.

Manufacturers

The establishment of a direct online link between manufacturer and consumer is advantageous to both. Customers get access to the manufacturer's full range of products—potentially for lower prices, as intermediaries do not skim part of the margin—and to their expertise. In turn, by interacting directly with consumers, manufacturers learn more about their needs and preferences and how they use products. Importantly, the money clawed back from retailers' margins can be used to help build the necessary, new sales capabilities.

The power of e-channels for manufacturers does not mean physical stores will cease to be important for them. Stores will continue to be a venue for showcasing brands and managing consumers' experience of them. But there is no doubt that manufacturers are no longer wholly reliant on traditional retailers as intermediaries. Box 5.2 describes how consumer goods company Procter & Gamble (P&G) has redefined its sales strategy to include online sales to end-users.

Logistics providers

Logistics providers such as the US Postal Service are building on their logistics expertise to step outside their core business and become retailers. DHL in Germany has its own online shopping platform, Meinpaket.de, which sells a range of products from various retailers and features product reviews, grouped around themes such as "technology and entertainment" or "living and enjoying." It delivers either to the customer's home, to the

Box 5.2 P&G's direct store

P&G, one of the world's largest consumer goods companies, launched its "eStore" in 2010. Besides featuring pages, or "stores," for key P&G brands such as CoverGirl and Gillette, the website provides services such as Pampers DiaperSizer, an online application to find the right diaper size by entering a baby's age, size, and weight, and LiveChat, whereby a consultant helps customers choose products from P&G's range. Functions such as "You may also like" foster cross-selling, while customers can interact and provide feedback via product reviews or by sharing tips and tricks. Furthermore, the e-commerce platform is linked to P&G's social-media presence, enabling users to access the eStore directly from the social media fan pages of P&G brands. A $5 flat rate for standard shipping and free shipping for orders of more than $25 round out the deal.

The eStore is owned and operated by PFSweb, an e-commerce and fulfillment services provider that manages order processing and distribution, while P&G provides the inventory and focuses on marketing and merchandising.

Source: Zak Stambor, "Procter & Gamble takes a step forward in online retailing," *Internet Retailer*, January 15, 2010, http://www.internetretailer. com/2010/01/15/procter-gamble-takes-a-step-forward-in-online-retailing, accessed January 23, 2013.

nearest post office, or to the closest parcel station, which can be accessed around the clock (Exhibit 5.9).

Some logistics providers could help new retailers enter the market. Shutl, an online portal in the United Kingdom, matches the excess capacity of local logistics providers with retailing demand (Box 5.3). This service can enable retailers of all hues to fulfill their orders rapidly, but it might be of particular interest to new retailers that want to parcel out aspects of their business.

Exhibit 5.9 Logistics players become retailers.
Source: Meinpaket.

Magazines

Technology is enabling new players that previously were not even part of the retailing supply chain to use their consumer connections to become retailers. Many people are already accustomed to paying their broadband provider for downloading films and TV series, for example. More recent is the move into e-commerce by glossy magazines. Bricks-and-mortar stores that hitherto regarded magazines as a place in which to advertise now face some as direct competitors.

Magazines engaging in what is often dubbed "editorial commerce" include *Vogue*, which through its publisher Condé Nast has formed an alliance with Moda Operandi, an e-commerce site from which new designer clothing collections can be preordered.[11] *GQ*, also published by Condé Nast, has entered a partnership with Gilt Man's new retail spinoff, Park & Bond. And the men's magazine *Details* works with Mr Porter, a website for men's designer clothing. In an interview with the *New York Times*, David Granger, editor-in-chief at *Esquire*, summed up the rationale for such moves: "What magazines have always done is to create desire in

Box 5.3 Shutl matching supply and demand

Shutl is an on-demand delivery company that connects Main Street (high street) retailers with local courier companies to deliver customers' online and in-store orders. During the checkout process, customers can choose between "Shutl now" (delivery to customer's home or office within the next 90 minutes) and "Shutl later" (booking a later, one-hour delivery slot and getting a real-time quote for delivery costs). The price for the Shutl service starts at £4.95 ($7), comparable to the price of standard delivery in the United Kingdom, and the service operates 24 hours a day, all year round.

How does it work? Shutl aggregates delivery capacities across a network of local same-day couriers, matching individual delivery requests to the optimum courier. Independent courier companies upload their prices into Shutl's system in order to bid automatically on local deliveries from retail partners. Instead of using a centralized warehouse system, Shutl coordinates the fulfillment of customers' online orders from the local outlets of the relevant retailers.

The service was initially tried out in London in cooperation with Argos, a leading Main Street retailer, and now extends to a number of metropolitan areas in the United Kingdom and a range of retailers such as the fashion chains Karen Millen, Oasis, and Warehouse and the electronics chain Maplin (Exhibit 5.10). Retailers benefit by extending their customer base, improving conversion rates on online sales, and reducing the cost of returns due to failed deliveries.

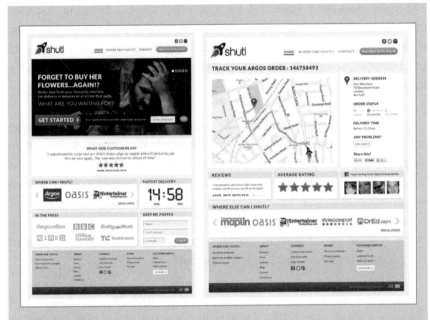

Exhibit 5.10 Shutl service options.
Source: Shutl's website.

Sources: Shutl, "About Shutl," http://www.shutl.co.uk/about, accessed January 23, 2013; Mike Butcher, "Shutl rolls out one hour online delivery service to six more UK cities," *TechCrunch*, October 4, 2011, http://techcrunch. com/2011/10/04/shutl-rolls-out-one-hour-online-delivery-service-to-6-more-uk-cities/, accessed January 23, 2013.

consumers. The next logical step is to fulfill that desire by selling the product. If we don't do it, somebody else is going to."[12]

Consumers

Then there are consumers themselves, often overlooked as "new players" but dominating an increasing proportion of online sales by selling products and services directly to each other, either through auctions or at a set price. These deals were once conducted through newspaper advertisements and specialist trading publications, bringing together the seller and buyer without a retailing intermediary. The difference now is that they are done at far greater scale, extending the seller's reach and the buyer's choice but also making it easier for both parties to find a trading partner.

In the United States and Europe, consumer-to-consumer (C2C) sales are already common. In 2011, US e-commerce was worth $194 billion, roughly 10 percent of which (some $20 billion) was C2C trade.[13] The biggest player in C2C in the United States and Europe is eBay, whose e-commerce revenues reached $12 billion in 2011, some 42 percent of which was estimated to be C2C trade.[14] Its market share in the United States was around 3 percent that year, and in Germany and the United Kingdom, it was between 13 and 15 percent.[15]

In Asia, C2C is bigger still. C2C business took hold in Asia before business-to-consumer (B2C) models in the early days of e-commerce, when companies were still hesitant to make the necessary investments. In China, the C2C market was worth $96 billion in 2011—more than four times bigger than the US market. Moreover, it accounts for nearly 80 percent of the total online retail market in China, having grown at an average annual rate of 87 percent since 2005.[16] The biggest player in the C2C market in China is Taobao, which enjoyed a market share of over 90 percent in 2011.[17]

Other variations of C2C markets also are emerging, facilitating the sale of unused or underused goods. Known as collaborative consumption, the movement has a green element for some practitioners. When consumers share, lend, or rent more products to one another, less is produced and wasted. But for some practitioners, there can be a clear profit motive, too.

Here, too, the concept may not be entirely new. Marketplaces for unused or underused goods have always existed, as thriving trunk (car boot) sales demonstrate. But what has changed is the way digital platforms are enhancing the efficiency of those marketplaces. One approach consists of community-based platforms that urge local people to share, such as Streetbank, a UK website that showcases the items and skills that neighbors are giving away, lending, or sharing—an attic, garden shed, drill, phone charger, or writing skills. But bigger businesses are profiting, too. Netflix has more than 20 million subscribers in the United States who essentially pay a fee to share DVDs, and Zipcar's more than 670,000 members share cars part-time. On a smaller scale, Airbnb allows people to rent their homes or even a room to travelers.

C2C platform providers typically make money by selling advertising, and some own third-party providers to facilitate secure online payments and an additional source of revenue. In this case, customers profit from higher security and simpler and faster payment transactions.

The power of information productivity

It is hard to overstate the extent to which big data has the power to transform retailers' operations. Huge and ever-greater quantities of information are now available to them, but unless retailers can find ways to deal with that information onslaught and extract what is meaningful, its utility is limited. On the positive side, as mentioned previously, a retailer using big data to the full can increase its operating margin by between 20 and 30 percent, and big data is expected to increase overall productivity in the US retail industry by an annual 0.5 percent over the next ten years.[18] Intelligent exploitation of these tools will be critical if retailers are to compete effectively in the future. Information productivity—that is, the ability to wring value from information—is becoming as important to value creation in the retail industry as the productivity of labor and capital.[19]

Retail has always been one of the most data-intensive industries. But despite the huge amount of information amassed, the value retailers could extract from it hitherto was limited for several reasons. First was the lack of granularity. Huge amounts of quite detailed data were available about the movement of thousands of different items, many times a year, from suppliers to warehouses and to store networks, and about the transactions of millions of customers. But as storage space was limited, much of the information available was lumped together in what is known as a batch process, with only the totals recorded for future analysis. Second, before the widespread use of customer loyalty cards and before the ability of retailers to interact with customers on the Internet, little was known about individual customers. There was no way of linking a sale to any one person. Retailers instead had to rely on the analysis of anonymous sales receipts for insights into customers' shopping habits, trends, and preferences. Third, even the available data was of limited use because of limited processing power needed to analyze large data sets. As a consequence, few retailers built the analytical skills and methodologies needed to unlock much value from the data.

Technology and big data have changed all that. Information can now be used both to improve operations and to establish much closer and more productive relationships with consumers, capturing their every transaction in the store and discovering more about them outside the store as well.

Owing to their lack of legacy systems and their "digital DNA," many online retailers may currently be best placed to collect and deploy data and reap the available rewards of information productivity. Still, there is hope for retailers that operate stores in addition to an online channel. As they learn, they may acquire an advantage in that they will be able to combine the richness of data they gather about their customers on the shop floor with data gathered online. Importantly, they will be able to use both kinds of data to react in real time—something that was once thought to be the preserve of online operators.

Progressive retailers show the way ahead

Leading retailers are already applying technology to raise information productivity across the value chain. Here are just a few examples:

Supply chain and inventory

Despite retailers' best efforts, retailing can remain inefficient, particularly in comparison with the controlled environment of factory manufacturing, due to the intrinsic characteristics of the business. Too often, shops are filled with buffer stock that is never required, and there are empty spaces on shelves, where sales are lost by default. A degree of inefficiency arises from the inherent variability of demand in the retail industry; some buffer stock is inevitable to meet variations in customer traffic. And some inefficiency exists because retailers have to purchase set quantities in return for certain procurement prices. But much inefficiency arises because of the complexity of the retail supply chain, whose many participants include manufacturers, suppliers, warehouse operators, distributors, store managers, and line managers. Technology is overcoming this.

To reap maximum value, retailers have always segmented the supply chain to find the right balance between service levels and logistics costs. For example, the frequency of shipments to the store, inventory levels, and transit time in a grocer's supply chain will be different for fresh and dry foods. Likewise, in an apparel retailer's supply chain, it will be different for the basic and high-fashion clothing collections. Real-time data, higher processing power, and more sophisticated algorithms mean a much finer segmentation is now possible. Not only is there far more data available about volumes, variability in demand, stock-outs, obsolescence, and handling and transportation costs, for example, but it can all be integrated and analyzed in a way that shows precisely the best balance between service levels and logistics on any number of products. One European retailer that "micro-segmented" the supply system in this way reduced total inventory volumes by 20 percent and total supply chain costs by 6 percent, while significantly improving product availability in its stores.

Closer collaboration across the entire supply chain by sharing real-time data on forecasts and inventories is also raising productivity. In 2012, Tesco launched Tesco Connect, a Web portal where suppliers can access not only Tesco's real-time inventory levels, information about current and planned promotions, and demand forecasts, but also the orders it foresees for the next two weeks on individual items. All this information helps suppliers plan ahead with near certainty for new orders *before* they are made, and they adjust production volumes, logistics, and priorities accordingly.

For the suppliers, this type of collaborative planning has huge, positive implications for their costs. But Tesco, too, reaps value. During the pilot stage of Tesco Connect, short or late deliveries from suppliers fell by more than a third. And knowing that suppliers had planned in accordance with its needs, Tesco reduced its own buffer stock in stores and warehouses and decreased stock-outs and lost sales.

Pricing and promotions

Figuring out how prices or promotions will affect sales has long been an inaccurate science, as consumers are influenced by so many different factors, including the magnitude of a price change, the prices charged by competitors, the importance of price on any given item for any given customer, and the traffic in the store. The list of variables is a long one.

In the past, commercial directors of grocery chains, for example, had to rely largely on basic, internal data and a good deal of experience, assumptions, and intuition to decide their strategies. Today, thanks to big data and sophisticated algorithms, they can simulate the effects of different pricing and promotional strategies by product category and estimate the resulting elasticity of demand with a high degree of accuracy. In addition, these algorithms can simulate the effects of external variables such as location, holiday periods, competitors' responses, and even the weather to make the predictive outcome even more accurate.

Retailers are thus enabled to answer questions such as these: Would it be better to increase the average rebate or the number of items on promotion? What competitive reaction is likely and, based on that, what is the optimal strategy? What caused a fall in actual sales from forecast ones?

Was it the price increase on private-label products, for example, or fewer promotions on fresh products, or both?

While statistical and mathematical algorithms have long been able to help answer such questions, again, lack of computing power has limited their use in retailing. This, too, is changing. One European retailer conducted this type of modeling to look at the effectiveness of its price and promotion strategy. It discovered that an investment equivalent to 1 percent of its gross margin would have the biggest impact on store sales and overall profitability if it increased the number of promotions rather than reducing prices. Another leading retailer conducted a similar analysis and learned that just 20 percent of its offers appeared to drive additional sales and loyalty. Applying this insight, it reduced the number of promotions it made in one month from 750 to 300 items. By better segmenting its customer base and making more tailored offers, it reduced its promotion expenses by £300 million.

Assortment optimization

Historically, retailers have defined the assortment based mainly on their experience and judgment, often following the advice of suppliers (who typically know the categories better) to add new products. Moreover, category managers typically have made decisions based on limited information (e.g. only basic facts on product volumes and margins) and basic rules (e.g. cut the least-profitable products from the assortment, but without assessing the impact on sales). Today, technology and advanced analytics allow retailers to take a huge step forward in assortment optimization. They can, for example, learn how consumers think about the category and hence how they make decisions in front of the shelf. For instance, consumers tend not to think in terms of the traditional and technical product label definition used by retailers to classify the assortment, such as water, carbonated drinks, juices, and alcoholic products, but more in terms of their own needs—a diet, organic, or sports drink, perhaps, or an aperitif. Retailers can also identify which consumer needs are unmet by the current assortment, discovering opportunities to increase sales by introducing new items. And they can assess the extent to which the introduction of a new product will cannibalize sales of another product, or the lost sales that will follow the delisting of a product.

How is this capability now possible? The first step is the collection of a broad set of data. Historical information about customers' buying habits can be collected from loyalty cards. But this is still not enough. It has to be supplemented with knowledge about consumer needs, attitudes, and behaviors, which can only be derived from qualitative and quantitative consumer surveys and market panels. Then technology and advanced analytics enable these insights and data to be combined to reveal a clear guide to assortment optimization and a quantitative assessment of sales and margins in alternative scenarios. Using such advanced analytics, one leading grocery retailer replaced 10 percent of low-margin products in its assortment with higher-margin ones, increasing sales by 2 percent and margins by 1 percent.

* * *

In summary, the role of the physical store needs rethinking in an age when consumers are no longer dependent upon stores. New players are rapidly emerging to meet the more stringent demands and changing shopping needs of today's consumers. And information productivity looks set to be a critical component of any retailer's future success. In Chapter 6, we examine what we see as the inevitable fallout from these three trends: the emergence of a new, limited set of business archetypes that will prove to be effective in the digital era.

Notes

1. This is true in terms of being able to reach consumers via their website. However, distance may limit their catchment area due to delivery costs and logistics.

2. Best Buy, "*Kiosk locations*," http://www.bestbuy.com/site/Store-Locator/Kiosk/pcmcat259500050000.c?id=pcmcat259500050000, accessed January 23, 2013.

3. McKinsey iConsumer retail survey 2010, "iConsumer U.S. 2010: Retail," p. 36.

4. Eataly, "Location and hours," http://www.eataly.com/locations-and-hours, accessed January 23, 2013.

5. Ipsos survey, September 2012. Results available at "Six in ten Americans prefer shopping in-store to buying online," *Marketing Charts*, December 6, 2012, http://www.marketingcharts.com/wp/interactive/6-in-10-americans-prefer-shopping-in-store-to-buying-online-25244/, accessed January 23, 2013.

6. GfK Consumer Scan, *Wertschöpfung statt Mengenwachstum*, 31 (Unternehmersespräch Kronberg 2012, GfK SE, Nürnberg, 2012).

7. Olivier Dauvers in partnership with A3 Distribution, "Drive insights 2013," shared by authors.

8. IDEO, "Retail experience redesign for Warnaco," http://www.ideo.com/work/retail-experience-redesign/, accessed January 23, 2013.

9. Maria Hunstig, "Adidas Neo sets up ten stores in Germany," *Sportswear International*, February 16, 2012, http://www.sportswearnet.com/businessnews/pages/protected/ADIDAS-NEO-SETS-UP-TEN-STORES-IN-GERMANY_4991.html, accessed January 23, 2013.

10. Roger Cheng: "Apple's new Grand Central store: It's experience, not the product," December 9, 2011, *CNET News*, http://news.cnet.com/8301-13579_3-57340268-37/apples-new-grand-central-store-its-the-experience-not-the-product/, accessed January 23, 2013.

11. Moda Operandi, "Meet the Moda Operandi team," http://modaoperandi.com/about-us/, accessed January 23, 2013.

12. Eric Wilson: "Magazines begin to sell the fashion they review," *New York Times*, September 25, 2011, http://www.nytimes.com/2011/09/26/business/media/magazines-begin-to-sell-the-fashion-they-review.html?_r=2&pagewanted=1, accessed January 23, 2013. *Esquire* sells fashion products online.

13. E-commerce estimate from US Commerce Department; C2C estimate based on eBay annual report, Forrester Research, Online Retail Forecast, 2011–2017, and sales of smaller players.

14. EBay annual report; Forrester Research, Online Retail Forecast, 2011–2017.

15. EBay annual report; Forrester Research, Online Retail Forecast, 2011–2017.

16. Macquarie Equities Research; iResearch, "2011–2012 China e-commerce report," brief ed., available at iresearchchina.com; Euromonitor International.

17. iResearch quoted by Li & Fung Research, "China's online retailing market, 2011," October 2011, available at http://www.funggroup.com/eng/knowledge/research/china_dis_issue90.pdf, accessed January 23, 2013.

18. James Manyika *et al.*, "Big data: The next frontier of innovation, competition, and productivity," McKinsey Global Institute, May 2011, http://www.mckinsey.com/insights/mgi/research/technology_and_innovation/big_data_the_next_frontier_for_innovation, accessed January 23, 2013.

19. There is strong empirical evidence that this is indeed the case. According to an MIT study (2008) many industries, including retail, show the same pattern, namely that the performance gap between information usage leaders and laggards within an industry is increasing. McAfee, "Blabla," MIT, (2008).

Chapter 6

The Future of Retail

*Co-authored with
Lis Hannemann-Strenger*

As we have shown, technology has eroded the monopoly that traditional, store-based retailers enjoyed as the intermediaries between suppliers and consumers. As a consequence, it has empowered consumers and enabled new competitors to emerge. But the news is not all bad. Technology has also presented opportunities to achieve greater heights of productivity and offer customers new experiences. Nevertheless, many retailers struggle to see beyond the fact that technology has struck a blow to the heart of their old business model, the physical store.

The store will continue to play an important role, but for traditional retailers to continue delivering value to consumers in the digital era, they will have to rethink their business models and transform their operations. What forms are these new models likely to take? Focusing on strategies for mainstream retailers (specifically, those that include in their mix large networks of stores and/or generate equivalent volumes of sales online), we have identified seven "archetypes" for the digital era that can be operated at scale, either by retailers with their roots in physical stores or by pure online operators. Some archetypes require just a few tweaks to existing retail models; some call for a more extensive or even radical makeover. Most importantly, each has a sharp value proposition, demanding particular skills and capabilities, that targets a specific need or desire of empowered consumers in the digital era. Without such a focus, the chances of enduring success are limited.

Stand-alone archetypes

In the first four archetypes, retailers address a particular core customer need relating to price, convenience, or breadth of choice. This focused approach generates four possible stand-alone models: lowest cost, convenience–location, convenience–preselection, and platform operator.

Lowest cost

It might be hard to imagine how future retailers could undercut today's fiercest price discounters, but undercut they will if they can combine the four features of this archetype: accurate forecasting, perfect integration of online and offline channels, small stores, and lean, scaled-up operations. The customers this archetype targets are those on tight budgets and those with an eye for a bargain who are shopping to replace everyday items. One attraction of this archetype is that the price and quality transparency afforded by technology has increased the numbers of bargain-hungry shoppers.

Retailers adopting this archetype will need to improve the accuracy of their demand forecasts. With precise, detailed forecasting, retailers can reap productivity gains in just about every area of store operations: coordinating staffing levels with customer traffic, cutting back waste of fresh food products and shrinkage (the percentage of products lost between the manufacturer and the point of sale), reducing stock-outs, and optimizing inventory space.

Integration of online and offline channels enables the retailer to outsource as many activities as possible to the customer. When consumers are part of the process, prices can fall, and demand forecasts can improve. Preordering is the key for this. Stores would therefore offer the best discounts to customers who are prepared to order online but forgo home delivery, instead visiting the store at a specified time to collect their goods from the shelves. So that customers can find items quickly without assistance, the retailer can e-mail them exact details of the items' locations in the store. Self-checkout or online payment in the store would further trim costs.

Reducing the size of stores would help to cut back on building, staff, and inventory expenses. Some retailers might even consider "dematerializing" to the extent that some stores become merely a depot for collecting orders—a move already made by a French grocery retailer. These "dark stores," as they are sometimes known, are significantly smaller than regular stores and not open for customers. They require staff, rather than the customer, to select and pack items, incurring the related operating costs. The ability to make this model more economical than running an actual store will depend on the retailer. It might prove to be an opportunity for logistics companies. Even if they have no knowledge of running stores or merchandising, they know about optimizing supply chain flows and running single-item picking processes—that is, fulfilling orders that consist of multiple articles, each in a quantity of one. They would need to add a digital interface with the customer, but this is a relatively straightforward task, given the availability of tested front-end solutions for online shops.

The lowest-cost archetype will require considerable scale to negotiate the lowest prices with suppliers so the store operators will be able to run the leanest of processes at scale and keep them that way. They must also offer reliable, consistent service, assuring availability of the products as promised during the preordering procedure. Technology will help these retailers manage the processes, interfacing with customers and optimizing the assortment—essentially, preselecting a narrow but relevant range for the customer, something that today's successful heavy discounters already do well.

Is there a pure online version of this archetype? Today's online heavy discounters tend to depend for their supplies on gray-market merchandise. Gray markets, which exist in various nonfood categories, involve stock that is surplus, either because manufacturers have produced too much, owing to inaccurate forecasts of demand (as occurs with consumer electronics), or because minimum order sizes force some retailers to order more than they can sell (as is common in the wristwatch business). The lower purchase price for the merchandise offsets the delivery costs to buyers. The extent to which this model can be scaled up is limited, though, given manufacturers' desire to restrict the volume of merchandise sold through these kinds of channels.

Another variant of this archetype is the consumer-to-consumer (C2C) platform, such as eBay, which consumers use for hunting down what they want at the best possible price. Low prices here often fail to reflect true costs, however. Sellers tend not to factor in their own time and expenses. Or in a situation where a small-business owner acquires gray-market merchandise, the manufacturer absorbs the discount. The potential for any single seller to scale up this model is limited if goods are sold or sourced in this way. For the platform operator, of course, the many small sales commissions it receives can add up to a sizable revenue stream.

The drawback of these platforms from a customer's point of view is that they can raise concerns about security and quality. Will the goods be shipped after the customer has paid for them? Will they be of the advertised quality? Might they be fake? C2C providers are introducing systems designed to mitigate such risks. EBay encourages buyers to rate sellers according to their reliability; China's Taobao partners with Alipay, a provider of online payment solutions that also serves as a kind of trustee in the interest of buyers (Alipay pays out the buyer's money only after no dispute between buyer and seller has arisen during an established settlement time). In China, moreover, the buyer has the right to open delivered goods and decide whether to accept them while the delivery person waits.[1]

Convenience–location

For decades, "location, location, location" was the retailer's mantra. In the future, it will remain so only for those operating convenience stores.

Convenience stores save consumers from making much effort to buy what they need or desire, although the ease of purchase comes at a price. For certain inexpensive categories of goods, people are often prepared to pay more at a local convenience store if it means they can avoid traveling further afield or waiting for an online delivery. And convenience stores are the quickest way of getting what you want—particularly important when you have forgotten a key ingredient for a meal.

The success of the convenience–location archetype depends on carefully chosen locations and appropriate size and layout of the stores. Stores in the operator's network need to be close to a good flow of potential customers and apart from competitors. Ideal locations might be in villages without another shop within five miles, at gas stations on busy commuter routes, or in airports. Stores will be relatively small—not just because rents are high in prime locations but also because convenience demands that customers be able to find their way around quickly. A simple layout, easy visibility of products, and fast checkouts speed the shopping process.

As with many other offline formats, the convenience model can encourage impulse purchases with appealing storefronts, signage, and promotional displays. Product category and assortment are important, too. Few people are affluent enough to choose convenience over price for expensive items such as top-of-the-line flat-screen televisions. But within lower-price categories, there are still plenty of choices to be made in order to maximize sales and profitability. Retailers will need to tailor their assortment to local consumers' needs and profiles, considering how much more they can charge than lower-cost retailers further afield or online sellers. They will also have to think about where digital might invade: newspapers and magazines, for example, look vulnerable.

Two trends suggest a promising future for the convenience–location archetype. First, in large Western cities, residents are starting to reconsider the need to own a car, and car ownership rates, particularly among younger people, are expected to drop. These consumers will thus have to rely more on local shops, particularly for everyday groceries. Second, and not unrelated, some consumers are consciously starting to support their local neighborhoods and businesses in preference to larger, out-of-town stores, valuing the sense of community and social interaction. With aging, less-mobile populations in many Western countries, this role might be reinforced.

We could see some interesting variants of this convenience store emerging. One possibility is a premium variant targeting affluent shoppers who are more interested in environmental considerations or the perceived quality of the produce than in the lower prices charged by bigger super- or hypermarkets. Some retailers are starting to offer "networked convenience," whereby goods bought at an airport store, for example, can be picked up from a sister store in the arrival airport rather than carted on and off the plane. Others offer unconnected services but a degree of convenience by allowing shoppers to complete several tasks at the same time. In Japan, for instance, shoppers at 7-Eleven stores can use printing machines to print photos, travel tickets, and even legal documents, and they can obtain catalog order forms, tax payment facilities, and postal services at the counter.[2]

Convenience–preselection

The second convenience archetype centers on choice and service. These elements could be said to describe the current value proposition of many big retail stores such as hypermarkets, department stores, and the big-box specialists. They offer convenience not in the form of proximity but in having everything under one roof. At the same time, they promise low—but not the lowest—prices and a high level of service, making it simple for customers to return goods or organize home delivery of large items. In its current guise, however, the choice-and-service model looks vulnerable, given the much wider choice available at competitive prices online and the relative convenience of online shopping. For many physical retailers that currently operate a choice-and-service model, a fall of just 10 percent in customer traffic could make their store economics unsustainable.[3]

The new physical version of this model therefore delivers convenience by offering choice that is limited but carefully crafted to meet customers' needs. Retailers offer buyers the convenience of knowing that the store will select the items that meet their requirements, saving them from the need to compare the differences among dozens of online options. A consumer electronics retailer, for example, might offer not 30 different 32-inch-screen televisions with dozens of features but just three that best suit the store's particular customers: perhaps one for technical geeks, another at a midrange, value-for-money price, and a third at an entry-level price. The traditional retailing task of preselection and choosing the right "editorial signature," discussed in Chapter 2, becomes more crucial than ever. Importantly, while prices might not be rock bottom, the archetype still requires that they be attractive.

With preselection actively communicated as a benefit to the consumer, the value proposition should be easily extendable to personalized services. Examples of personalized services with potentially high margins for the retailer include home delivery, project support (e.g. setting up the Wi-Fi network at home or building a pond in the garden), and product leasing with automatic updates (e.g. "renting" a tablet computer and getting a new version as soon as it is available).

Stocking a smaller assortment of goods has many advantages. Stores can be smaller, delivering lower operating and staffing costs and greater leeway to compete on price with online operators. The retailer can carry larger volumes of each item, giving the company more negotiating power with manufacturers and room to lower prices still further. And it might have room to increase sales of its private-label goods, helping to avoid direct price comparisons. Reducing the size of the assortment can also make it easier to identify the best products, promotions, and services for targeted customers, and to develop new ones. These superior insights are an important element of the value proposition, as customers need to trust the retailer to understand and fulfill their shopping needs.

To enable retailers to make the right selection, decision-support systems are essential. These systems use detailed selling data, external data (be they weather forecasts or information on competitors' actions), and customer data such as information on loyalty cards and details about consumers' online behavior (e.g. search patterns on Google) to forecast demand for new products. Technology will also influence how the store communicates with customers. A "smart shelf" that reaches out to the customer in front of it via his or her smartphone, pointing to the offers most relevant to that customer, may become the norm. Or the store will change what is displayed on its digital signage according to the time of day and the customer mix in the store. During midmorning in a grocery store, the signage may focus on attractive deals for young mothers. An apparel store detecting a large group of teenagers in the store may display promotional ads starring the latest teen star instead of a video from a fashion show in Paris. Given that online channels are becoming synonymous with convenience, physical retailers choosing this model will also have to offer shoppers an online channel and the option of carrying home purchases from the store or having them delivered.[4] Technology should enable the consumer to go online to get real-time information about items in stock at the nearest outlet or store-only deals.

The online channel should also support the notion of providing a solution "designed for your needs." Even in grocery, this is possible. Imagine that the website of your favorite grocer would help you prepare your shopping list for tonight's family dinner by guiding you through a selection that runs like this: "below $20 for four → organic meats only → maximum cooking time 30 minutes → special requirement: no peanuts → seasonal vegetables," and so on. The resulting shopping list is stored on your smartphone, and together with the aisle map it can access on site, it will guide you efficiently through the store. The key here is that the different channels are perfectly integrated so that they drive traffic and business to one another.

There is, however, an alternative to perfectly integrated channels, and that is to use a variety of front ends on the same back end. The US kitchenware, furniture, and linens retailer Williams-Sonoma has finessed such a model. Instead of simply replicating the offline store online, it has different websites for different customer segments, as well as six different catalogs, enabling it to reach more customers and test new products and brands before bringing them into its stores.[5]

Catalog companies, which started life back in the 19th century, successfully offer this kind of edited choice without operating stores: their catalogs bear their editorial signature. Online players can adopt this archetype, too. Our view is that the pure breadth of the product mix will come to matter less and less. Indeed, retailers that offer an excessively broad selection might weaken their value proposition if consumers come to see too much choice as a disadvantage and prefer to be guided in their selections. Either they will visit shops and online sites that preselect for them or they will make their choice, based on information from (digital) friends or customer reviews, before purchasing online from whichever retailer has the item at the cheapest price.

Whether pure online players or those that also own physical stores come to be the better exponents of this archetype remains to be seen. Physical retailers can always outclass pure online operators when it comes to meeting consumers' desire for instant gratification, and online shopping can come with a measure of inconvenience, be it arranging a time for delivery or returning goods. Physical retailers also have the advantage of being able to offer a more personal level of service. At the same time, though, consumers enjoy the convenience of shopping on their computer or tablet screens, and flexible logistics providers are improving delivery services (see Chapter 4). Consumers will certainly, therefore, reward the online player that knows its consumers well enough to tailor the perfect assortment of products for sale.

Platform operator

Despite the importance of preselection, we are not arguing that there is no longer a place for the choice-and-service model, only that its place is threatened in the physical world. Consumers will still buy at online sites that offer a vast assortment of goods because they are likelier to find the exact item they have chosen already, possibly at a very good price and with convenient order handling and delivery.

The digital-era version of the choice-and-service model is the platform operator, epitomized by Amazon. This type of retailer is strikingly similar to its physical predecessors: it prides itself on its range of goods, offers services such as search tools and a simple checkout process, guarantees a certain standard of quality (e.g. Amazon closely monitors the customer feedback on its marketplace sellers), and sets attractive prices (though not rock bottom). The digital version is superior, however, as it offers a still wider choice and a still better, easier-to-use selection and payment service.

The biggest hypermarkets and even entire shopping malls have a rather narrow assortment compared with the choice offered by an online platform operator the size of Amazon, which, in addition to its own inventory, sells other retailers' goods. In addition, Amazon offers a recommendation function that helps customers find what they want based on their previous shopping behavior. The information counter at a shopping mall looks almost derisory in comparison.

The economic attraction of this model lies not so much in revenue generated from the platform operator's own inventory sales. These sales could be the least attractive part of the business, given that they expose the retailer to price competition and the risk of holding unsold inventory. Rather, it lies in the commission and handling fees charged by the operator to third-party retailers for access to customers, logistics capabilities, and the setting of quality standards.

Technology and innovation are fundamental to this archetype, which is already helping new competitors reach consumers. Manufacturers, for example, can use the established front end of a platform operator to establish a business-to-consumer (B2C) function.

Building on the stand-alone models

The next three archetypes—experience, exclusivity, and ecosystem—are variants of the stand-alone models, adding another dimension to them (Exhibit 6.1). They give consumers additional reasons to shop that go beyond the basics of price, convenience, and preselection. So, for example, the lowest-cost archetype may add an exclusivity dimension, or the convenience–preselection archetype an experience element, using the latest 3D display technology to showcase the products or their application.

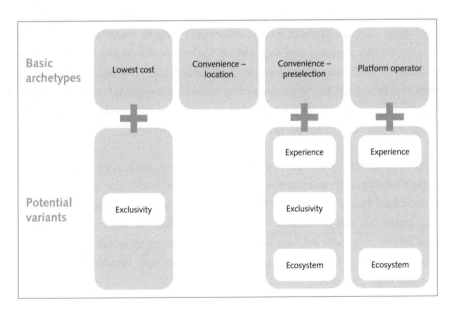

Exhibit 6.1 Variants of retail archetypes with potential for success at scale.

Experience

The experience archetype satisfies people's natural inclination to see and touch before buying—something online players struggle to match. Going a step further, it offers consumers an opportunity to shop as a means of entertainment and social interaction.

Even for established store operators, when it comes to providing an experience, the bar has been raised. Few shopping malls or department stores today offer much that visitors would describe as entertaining, so accustomed are they to most of what is on offer. Malls are often no more than a collection of clothing and jewelry stores with a few restaurants and the odd consumer electronics retailer or bookstore. In addition, customers now weigh the experience of a shopping trip against the convenience and choice of shopping online, where many spend hours interacting with friends and family.

In the digital era, we believe, physical stores wanting to differentiate themselves through the experience they offer will need to set the bar so high that their customers would effectively pay to enter the store. This requirement rules out the experience archetype for many retailers. But certain formats can charge prices that cover the cost of investment in fixtures, furniture, technical wizardry, and sales personnel trained to build relationships with consumers. Moreover, all these enhancements help trigger in-store purchases, including impulse buys.

Those relationships can be improved further with sophisticated customer relationship management programs. The better the insights about customers' tastes, the tighter the relationship and the higher the switching costs for the consumer. No consumer likes to start from scratch, describing to a new retailer her preferences, such as what kind of jeans she likes. And it takes many purchases before a new retailer can identify the relevant patterns.

It will be hard for retailers to replicate the store experience in an online channel, designed as it is around the physical touch and feel of products, personal advice, and store ambience. Indeed, the brand image and the price premium it can command might be undermined by a purely transactional website. But an online presence remains a must for engaging consumers, providing relevant information, and driving customer traffic to stores. It will even enhance the sales of a brand whose reputation has been built upon the in-store experience—particularly because the website can serve cities or countries not covered by the store network and can offer more items than stores might have space for. Store staff can enhance the link between the store and the online shop by using in-store devices to help customers order items that are not in stock.

The main threat to the experience model is customer empowerment. With information about products and prices at their fingertips, wherever they might be, customers can enjoy a trip to the store but then order online for less or even negotiate a lower price in the store. Store retailers can take various measures, including personalized interaction with sales assistants, to help prevent this showrooming and encourage a sale. US-based Nordstrom, for example, is testing iPads at its bridal shops and special-occasion dress departments in several stores. Sales assistants rely on the iPads to help customers search for dresses in colors and styles that are unavailable in one store but may be available in another. Efforts to promote impulse purchases through product display and demonstrations also boost turnover. But prices still have to be competitive. If these retailers cannot come close to matching prices in categories where specialist, online operators enjoy huge economies of scale, they might have to consider not competing in them. And where they do compete, they will have to manage prices more actively than many retailers do today, perhaps by adjusting them within a day to match offers available from online retailers.

Another way to prevent showrooming is to limit the scope of online comparisons by investing in exclusive and store-branded merchandise. Department stores have long collaborated with famous designers to develop exclusive product lines. Today, other types of stores, including specialists such as electronics retailers, increasingly see the value in exclusivity.[6] Taken to an extreme, exclusivity becomes an archetype in its own right, and is discussed next.

Exclusivity

The exclusivity archetype is built on uniqueness: customers know that if they want a certain product or brand there is only one place to buy it. The allure for retailers is twofold: they escape direct price comparisons, as the same cannot be bought elsewhere, and they control all aspects of the value chain relevant to the customer, as they influence or even decide outright the characteristics and price positioning of the products they sell. An exclusive retailer can also control the marketing strategy, rather than depending on a manufacturer's advertising or image. Although exclusivity is often associated with brands that convey luxury, a certain lifestyle, or even social status, the archetype lends itself to brands across a range of price levels, as mass-market clothing labels such as Zara, H&M, and Abercrombie & Fitch attest. In fact, almost all the items sold by the low-cost supermarket operator Aldi are private-label ones.

As ever, technology will reveal customer insights for improving products and services, defining prices, promotions, and marketing campaigns and services that improve the customer's experience and fulfill the brand's unique promise. For some exclusive retailers, the shopping experience will be crucial to success, and retailers must constantly innovate to provide great experiences. In Box 6.1, we show how Burberry, an example of the exclusivity archetype, has given its store in Beijing a digital makeover in order to offer a unique experience.

Burberry's move illustrates an understanding that even for luxury goods—a category that many believed would be slower to go digital because people would always want to see expensive goods first and soak up the exclusive in-store experience—digital sales can be a strong source of growth. Research between McKinsey and Altagamma, the trade association for Italian luxury goods companies, in 2012 showed that "pure"

Box 6.1 Burberry's digital makeover

At the opening of its flagship store in Beijing in April 2011, Burberry promoted its tech-savvy credentials to young Chinese people by staging a fashion show that included hologram-projected models interacting with live models (Exhibit 6.2). The aim of the glamorous event was to connect the brand with some of the world's most digitally empowered consumers, CEO Angela Ahrendts told the *Wall Street Journal*.

Exhibit 6.2 Burberry's Beijing runway event.
Source: http://www.youtube.com/watch?v=9t5dCIuz2wY.

In the stores, mirror-sized touch-screen displays and Apple iPads give shoppers access to Burberry's full collection, while giant LED screens show Burberry videos. It is retailing as theater. The aim is to enable customers to buy at any time, in any place, in any fashion, offline or online.

Source: Laurie Burkitt, "Burberry stores in China get digital makeover," *Wall Street Journal*, April 13, 2011.

online sales already account for over 3 percent of the global luxury goods market, and up to 11 percent of offline sales are directly influenced by consumers' online experience (i.e. consumers were not sure they would make a purchase before going online, or they changed their minds about what to buy once there).[7] The challenge for the retailer is to integrate online and offline channels perfectly and to convey exclusivity, via consistent messages, at every contact with the customer.

For pure online operators basing themselves on the exclusivity model, it is hard to rival multichannel counterparts: part of the value proposition depends upon the physical, in-store experience. But it is not impossible. Some pure online players use a Web interface to design and deliver a customized product, be it a piece of furniture or a muesli mix. This kind of customization, albeit of the same basic products, still has an air of exclusivity, along with the opportunity to charge premium prices.

The pure online version of the exclusivity model might also suit manufacturers seeking to sell to consumers directly. By offering products that are not available in shops or on other websites, these companies can avoid conflict with retailers that might feel threatened by B2C sales.

Ecosystem

The ecosystem archetype is built around sales of a key product, or family of products, that is compatible only with—or at least works best with—additional goods and services bought through a channel controlled by the manufacturer, thus locking in the customer. This archetype results in limited competition and may allow high margins. Often, the retailer scales up the customer base by selling the core product relatively cheaply and the proprietary add-ons at relatively high prices.

Operators of this archetype include Apple for the iPod, iPhone, and iTunes; Nespresso with its coffee-brewing system; and Amazon with the Kindle publishing system. The concept stretches to other categories and applications. Take smart refrigerators, described in Chapter 3, which may give retailers and manufacturers all kinds of opportunities for providing replenishment services after the unit is installed.

Convenience is part of the value proposition of the ecosystem archetype: all the add-ons are controlled by a single provider that reliably delivers goods and services of high quality. Frequent innovations are likely, too. Thus, a key factor in the archetype's success will be the ability to manage the ecosystem, setting common business aims for all members of the supply chain and sharing the benefits and potential risks among them. Vertical integration will sometimes be the chosen course. Amazon, producer of the Kindle, is now offering the full range of publishing services, writing publishers out of the deal. As Russell Grandinetti, one of Amazon's top executives, said, "The only really necessary people in the publishing process now are the writer and reader."[8]

This archetype is suitable for pure online players in categories where touch and feel are, generally speaking, of less importance, as in the case of books. For other categories, stores are important in strengthening brand image and providing the shopping experience that many customers want and enjoy. Apple could exist without the Apple Stores, but the stores have palpable benefits for the brand. Likewise, Nespresso invested heavily in its own coffee shops when it discovered that consumers tend to prefer the taste of coffee drunk in pleasant surroundings, rather than, say, at a gas station or even at home, even when the drink is made in the same way with the same ingredients (Exhibit 6.3).

Understanding which archetypes are capable of serving customers' needs in the digital era—and, perhaps more importantly, understanding why—is an important first step for conventional, store-based retailers to take in evaluating their futures. But we are by no means suggesting this will suffice. Many retailers will find they need to transform their organizations, whichever archetype they might choose, to the extent that they become barely recognizable. They will need to change their processes, the staff they employ, the skills they need, and the way they approach their

Exhibit 6.3 Nespresso stores.
Source: Nepresso's website.

customers. Most importantly, they will need to change the way they think. Chapter 7 describes the transformation that must take place.

Notes

1. Zia Daniell Widger, "Trends in China's e-commerce market," Forrester Research, January 11, 2011.
2. McKinsey research.
3. Assuming a gross margin of 25 to 30 percent and an earnings before interest and taxes (EBIT) margin of 3 percent, a drop in customer traffic of 10 percent with no change in conversion or average ticket size more or less wipes out the EBIT contribution of the store network, as it is difficult to counter this shortfall with adequate reductions in operations expenditure.
4. See GSI Commerce, "2011 UK Fashion Retail Report," September 2011, p. 6.

5. McKinsey research.

6. Dana Mattioli, "Retailers try to thwart price apps," *Wall Street Journal*, December 23, 2011, http://online.wsj.com/article/SB1000142405297020368620457711 14901480554444.html, accessed January 23, 2013.

7. "Digital luxury experience 2012: From customer experience to impact," conference presentation, Altagamma-McKinsey Observatory, Milan, September 17, 2012.

8. David Streitfeld, "Amazon signs up authors, writing publishers out of deal," *New York Times*, October 16, 2011, http://www.nytimes.com/2011/10/17/technology/amazon-rewrites-the-rules-of-book-publishing.html?pagewanted =all&_r=0, accessed January 23, 2013. See also Tim Worsthall, "Amazon, Apple, and the perils of vertical integration," *Forbes*, April 23, 2012, http://www.forbes.com/sites/timworstall/2012/04/23/amazon-apple-and-the-perils-of-vertical-integration/, accessed January 23, 2013.

Chapter 7

A Call to Action

Co-authored with James Naylor

How prepared are today's retailers for the changes ahead and, in particular, the pace of change that technology is driving? In our experience, too many of those who began their careers operating stores are still trying to squeeze more from their traditional business processes rather than responding to the new world in entirely new ways. Their focus often remains on store openings, negotiations with suppliers to drive down prices, and other cost management measures. If sales are sluggish, they might have a go at more promotions or mine their loyalty card data to conduct a few one-off marketing campaigns. Any new, digital-related opportunities they decide to explore tend to be regarded as "projects," even though these are the very essence of their future identity and need to be pursued at scale.

Amazon's growth trajectory illustrates how out of date this thinking is. In the past decade, Amazon's revenues have grown by 32 percent a year on average, reaching $48 billion in 2011. With market capitalization in the region of $110 billion, Amazon is more highly valued than Target, Walgreens, and Kroger combined. Yet how many traditional store operators have come anywhere close to capturing the potential growth that digital commerce can deliver in all manner of categories, or even carefully considered what that potential might be?

If retailers fully grasped the pace of change and how it will affect their businesses, maybe their thinking and strategies would alter. Previous chapters have spelled out the significance of the change, but the point bears reinforcing with some examples. In McKinsey's 2011 iConsumer research, 66 percent of US consumers of electronics made the purchase online, up from 55 percent in 2010.[1] Even in the grocery sector, where many are still convinced that e-commerce will not work, there has been significant growth in the share of consumers who say they regularly shop online. In the United Kingdom, 17 percent of consumers did so in 2012, up from 11 percent in 2008.[2] The numbers in France (5 percent in 2010, versus 2 percent in 2007) and Spain (3 percent in 2010, versus 2 percent in 2007) are smaller but also trending upward.[3]

Awareness of the historical pace of change also needs to be combined with an eye to the future and the realization that the young people now on the threshold of becoming mainstream consumers are digital natives. By 2020, about 27 percent of Western Europe's population will have been born after 1980, amounting to 102 million consumers.[4] Unlike many of today's older consumers, this cohort uses digital technology almost intuitively and will surely accelerate the speed of change in retailing.

The fact that it takes time to build the skills required of a digital-era retailer also should be a prompt to immediate action. The few store-based retailers recognized for embracing the power of technology took almost a decade to transform their businesses. Retailers that have yet to begin the process no longer have the luxury of so much time, particularly as digital-era shoppers might prove to be loyal to the first movers. Although we argue that technology has empowered consumers by giving them more choice and transparency, loyalty still might develop in response to familiarity with a certain website, appreciation of the benefits a particular retailer offers (e.g. convenience or its understanding of an individual's shopping habits and preferences), or even the building of an emotional bond through an online community. How many of us are already loyal to certain portals simply because we are used to them?

Retailers yet to embark upon a transformation will need to accept that they must move much faster and thus more boldly than those currently at the forefront of change. There is undoubtedly a great deal to be learned from the experiences of technology pioneers and from observing how they work. But the time for a me-too approach is long gone.

Leapfrogging

The good news is that technological advances can make it easier for late-comers to make huge strides. In high-tech industries, innovation is inevitably technology related: a striking new development catapults the industry ahead, creating new industry leaders. An obvious example of leapfrogging is the Apple iPhone, which radically altered the nature of mobile phones by combining basic voice communication with Internet and multimedia capabilities, touch-screen functionalities, and a platform that could feed off a vast ecosystem that included iTunes and a stunning array of apps. Other companies have since followed Apple's lead, but the new technology dealt a serious blow to the fortunes of some leading mobile-phone manufacturers at the time of its introduction.

In retail, technology-driven innovation has been important, of course, but the pace has been slower. Now, in the digital era, we believe most retail innovation will be driven by technology, making the industry more akin to the high-tech sector and explaining why companies familiar with emerging technologies and equipped to embrace them can leapfrog ahead. As one senior executive of a global online retailer told us, "If I were forced to choose, I'd say we were a technology company rather than a retailer."

To make fast progress, retailers can choose from three different kinds of opportunity. Just by deploying the most recent innovations on the market today, such as cloud computing, retailers that have so far occupied the rearguard will be able to leap forward. In addition, given the pace of innovation and the potential of the new technologies, IT-backed solutions to retailing's challenges will quickly emerge and be way ahead of what even today's most digitally astute retailers have yet discovered. Finally, leapfrogging opportunities will arise from consumers' growing receptiveness to new ways of shopping. Developments in areas such as mobile, augmented reality, and social media will be used to target the next generation of digitally savvy consumers in entirely new, though as yet unknown, ways that many of today's consumers simply would not have an appetite for. The aspiration must be to avoid merely emulating today's digital leaders in retail but, rather, to move ahead of them.

The way forward

If store-based retailers are determined to transform their business and succeed in the digital era, what then do they need to do? There are three preliminary steps:

1. Shift the mental model.
2. Set a new aspiration for the business.
3. Adapt the organization.

Shift the mental model

Before the digital era, retailers enjoyed a privileged position as intermediaries between suppliers and consumers, controlling the physical flow of goods between them as well as the information flows required to match supply with demand. Their power as intermediaries was reinforced as they learned how to manage more complex operations and thus how to grow through territorial expansion, at home or abroad.

But that business model has been threatened as the emergence of new competitors and consumers' growing use of technology to take more control over purchasing decisions has blurred retail's boundaries. In addition, technology has supercharged information as a competitive weapon in retail.

In consequence, we believe that store-based retailers wanting to make their mark in the digital era need to refocus the mental model that has guided retailers' business thinking for centuries. This will require that retail organizations become customer-centric, digitally fluent, and super agile.

Customer-centricity

Most retailers will say they care about their customers. But caring about customers in the digital era takes on a whole new meaning. A better way to understand this concept is in terms of customer-centricity, which requires a different way of thinking.

Today, most retailing consists of preselecting large quantities of products that appeal to large numbers of customers and making them available in stores. Any mapping of the information flows in the retail systems that support this process quickly reveals them to be anchored in the world of products, not customers. All enterprise resource planning (ERP) systems, for example, essentially manage the flow of products.

By contrast, customer-centricity puts customers at the center of all operations. Many retailers already have loyalty programs and use the data collected to analyze consumer behavior and trends. But this does not make them customer-centric. Very few retailers continuously link the insights provided by the analysis with commercial processes. They do not, for example, modify the type of goods they sell, their prices, or their promotions upon discovering that the neighborhood of a certain store has a large ethnic population with different consumer habits or bigger or smaller families.

Likewise, few of the pieces of data collected from social networks and the Web are systematically used to establish relationships with consumers by providing personalized offers. Contrast this with the practices at some leading grocery retailers that are more customer-centric. Some, for example, collect data on the prices being offered by competitors every single day and change their own prices accordingly in order to guarantee their customers the best deals. Commercial directors in the vast majority of retailers would blanch if asked to provide this degree of responsiveness to customers. They would find it impossible.

But customer-centricity is essential if retailers are to remain competitive. Because technology enables them to know their customers so much better, it is evident that if some retailers fail to engage with consumers and serve them on the basis of that knowledge, a competitor will—not least because customers can so easily move between retailers.

In some respects, customer-centricity means returning to the kind of thinking that prevailed when owners of small stores bought the merchandise they knew individual customers would like. Retailers sacrificed this intimacy in favor of scale, as technology emerged to help them manage more complex operations more efficiently. But technology has moved on again. Now successful retailers can—indeed, must—get reacquainted with each of their customers *and* operate at scale. Customer-centricity will need to be valued not just by the store owner, as in the past, but by all employees in the organization and become embedded in their daily tasks.

Casino, the French grocery giant, is at the forefront of moves to invest in customer-centricity. It is able to engage consumers to the extent that it delivers personalized offers in real time across several channels. To do this, it has compiled a database that contains information reflecting customers' buying patterns based on their loyalty cards and online browsing activity. The result is a real-time marketing engine capable of making personalized recommendations and offers from among 500,000 different products. By downloading an app, Casino customers can create a shopping list from the online store, add further products at home by scanning the bar codes with their smartphone, and complete the order in a Casino store by scanning the tags of products on the shelves. At every stage, the marketing engine makes suggestions—additional ingredients for a recipe, tailored promotions, or recommendations for complementary products— based on what is already in the shopping basket and the customer's profile. Finally, customers can check out quickly by scanning their smartphone at the cash register. As a result of installing these capabilities,

Casino says, it has seen a significant increase in the size of the average basket of goods.[5] Wal-Mart, too, is able to provide customers with a personalized promotion when they are at the checkout. Technology combines data collected from customers' loyalty cards with data from the items in their shopping baskets to produce, instantly, a voucher containing a set of relevant promotional offers.

A global clothing manufacturer and retailer offers another example of customer-centricity: it uses the Web to enable customers to design their own shoes. They can select from a variety of shapes, colors, laces, and prints and then buy the customized shoes online, picking them up from a store or taking delivery at home. In this way, the retailer offers an exclusive value proposition. Perhaps more importantly, it also gets to mine unique information about customers' preferences, whether or not they actually buy the shoes, which it can use as input for designing its collections.

How retailers use the ability constantly to capture and leverage customer-specific information is the new battleground for retail. Many, though, are not battle-ready—and will not be until they change their thinking about customers' place in their business model.

Digital fluency

Understanding the technology that supports the business and possessing the skills to use it were once necessary attributes for only a small group of managers in retail businesses. The majority concentrated on how to get the best from their suppliers or how new stores were performing. In the digital era, technological know-how will have to be far more pervasive if the organization is to understand the opportunities it offers and capture them. This is what we mean by digital fluency. It includes the following essential elements:

- **Platform awareness.** Many of the people in the organization will need to be familiar with all the different platforms their customers use—social media, blogs, or popular websites—as well as the manner in which they are used. No self-respecting manager in retail will be able to claim half-proudly that he or she does not get the point of Twitter or Facebook, or does not grasp how a complaint in a blog by a single customer can be rapidly amplified to put the company into the national spotlight. Commercial managers, as well as those below them, will need platform awareness just as much as any technology officer—not at an engineering level necessarily, but in terms of what it means for customers.

- **Regular engagement with customers.** In the past, retailers could engage with their customers only in their stores or through a handful of advertising channels. Today, there are many more channels and hence opportunities, particularly because consumers use the Internet so frequently, whether or not they are shopping. Wal-Mart, for example, posts fresh messages, photographs, and videos on Facebook five times a day. At the same time, the retail business model is moving away from communication push. In the digital era, communication must be a two-way conversation if it is to engage existing customers and create bonds and relationships with new ones. This, too, requires a change of mindset and represents a steep learning curve. Retailers need to learn how best to communicate with and engage different segments of consumers as well as individual ones, and they need to learn the right level of engagement: too low, and they risk losing customers to competitors; too high, and they risk annoying and, again, losing them. But whatever the right level (and it will differ depending on the category), the number of people able and authorized to communicate on behalf of the retailer in real time must increase sharply.

- **Analytical skills to support decision-making.** The huge amounts of data available to the retail organization of the future will be useless if the organization cannot analyze the data in order to draw conclusions for action that in turn engage customers and improve productivity. Analytics are not part of traditional retailers' DNA, though. Hence, many more people in the organization will have to possess not only basic mathematical and statistical knowledge but also higher-level filtering and problem-solving skills. With the help of advanced analytical tools, they will need to be able to prioritize and make sense of complex messages and their implications both for day-to-day decisions and the operating model of the business they work for, and to understand and feel comfortable with the rapid formation and testing of hypotheses.

Acquisition of agility

In the digital era, not only will companies have to be able to gather and analyze large amounts of data: they will have to be able to do so at speed and then hardwire the business insights into core processes faster than most will be accustomed to working. And all the while, they will need to keep abreast of new technological developments. The arrival of Amazon and other online competitors, whose success is partly built upon their ability to respond rapidly to all sorts of market signals, has shown the extraordinary power of agility as a strategic weapon in a technological environment. Many more companies in the retail industry will be compelled to build similar levels of agility if they are to remain competitive—able, for example, to react instantly to competitors' moves on pricing by collecting prices daily across all channels.

A prerequisite for agility is good data management. This might seem a mundane task, given the other challenges retailers face in transforming their operations. But many have inherited disparate data sets and systems as their companies have grown, or use different systems in different channels, so they cannot integrate their data in a way that facilitates data collection and interpretation. One company we know had more than 100 different legal entities with almost no integration of systems and processes. In a situation such as this, it is hard for different parts of the company to share information or learn from each other. For example, R&D may be able to see information about only the products in development, rather than the company's entire catalog, while sales and operations get to see only past sales volumes, so they cannot offer insights based on seeing business units' plans for the future. In addition, the independent information systems make it hard to get a meaningful company-wide view of even basic data such as sales or margins, let alone respond to market trends at the speed the digital era requires. The retailing clock has accelerated, and retailers will not keep pace without sound data management.

Good data management requires a system that ensures everyone in the organization has the same, unified view of data—whether it's data on customers, suppliers, or accounts, whatever the source—and is the basis for any agile and advanced decision-making. Given their starting positions, many retailers will have to change the way they work to manage data in this way. They might also have to upgrade their IT systems, although this could be required irrespective of data management if they are to integrate different channels and deploy new IT solutions quickly. Their legacy systems, along with fragmented applications and interfaces, make it hard to be agile, a fact no doubt reflected in the sharp, recent increase in IT spending in the retail industry. Some companies will need to replace their platforms entirely, some might choose to upgrade specific functions, and some might decide to integrate cloud-based services from various providers over a network-based architecture.

Set a new aspiration for the business

A successful transformation begins with clarity about what a company aspires to be. To this end, a retailer must understand how the paradigm shifts we describe are changing customers' behavior in its sector, segment, and geography; the competitive dynamics; and the potential impact on the economics of the current business model. A retailer also needs to understand the opportunities—the new ways to engage customers and capture cost efficiencies, for example, and the capabilities and skills required to do so.

With this contextual understanding, the different archetypes described in Chapter 6 might prove helpful in starting to shape the new aspiration and, from there, the business strategy. Their clarity and simplicity can help a company to consider whether its current value proposition is sound in the digital era or whether it will be forced to formulate a new one. Bear in mind that it is always easier to build distinctive propositions on current strengths than to try to build new strengths, but structural change may still be required. For example, a retailer that prides itself on knowing what customers want, based on their interaction with sales associates in its stores, might be hard-pressed to replicate that strength online. New skills and capabilities are likely to be required, as well as significant investment.

Each company's value proposition will be largely defined by a single archetype, perhaps with others to reinforce it. For example, a store-based retailer could decide to take advantage of its understanding of customers' needs and opt for the preselection archetype, knowing it can offer distinct value in the selection of goods. But it could also add an experience component to bolster the value proposition. Multi-format retailers will have to think through which archetype best suits different parts of their business. They might choose a different reference archetype for each one, but, as has always been the case, they will have to ensure that the overall brand strategy remains coherent.

Adapt the organization

With the broad direction of travel clear, retailers will have to adapt their organizations for the journey. We have already touched upon the need to change the company's mindset, which will have implications for the kinds of staff and skills required. Processes and organizational structures also must be adapted.

New staff and new skills

Digital fluency demands that technology be integrated into the thinking and capabilities of every part of management. All persons concerned with building the company's talent, from the CEO to operating leaders and human resources, have to accept the requirement to transform the way in which their teams talk, think, and work.

They might have to face the fact that some of the best-qualified teams are likely to be younger than many of their existing staff. Like it or not, young people are more familiar with the various technology platforms and more comfortable using them than older people are, which means they are better placed to understand the coming generation of digital consumers. Leveraging their talents will be important for retailers wanting to build a digitally fluent organization, and recruitment, training, and development processes might have to change to put younger people in more senior positions more quickly. Junior employees, such as store associates, will be expected to use digital devices to understand the product range and delivery options in order to raise the level of customer service, and we have already mentioned the need to manage fast-paced, online customer interactions. While these young employees will likely be technically literate, performing the customer-facing tasks that the technology enables will require a higher level of education than has conventionally been associated with lower-level retail positions.

New processes

Insights derived from big data and its analysis will have a profound effect on core business processes. For example, supply chain management will change if retailers choose to encourage customers to preorder and agree on a collection time as a way to improve forecasting accuracy and cut costs. Similarly, category management procedures, in the form of promotion and pricing management, will have to adapt to integrate digital and physical channels. Online channels can change a price in a fraction of a second to match competitors' prices, but how will stores be expected to respond, and how can that process be managed?

Communication processes also will be different if, for example, a retailer chooses an ecosystem archetype and has to find new ways of sharing information across the network. Performance management processes will need to be rethought to prevent the online channel from being a subscale silo that is the bottom of the priority list for buyers, an afterthought for the rest of the organization, and off the radar in stores.

To press home the importance of online channels, some retailers pay commissions to store personnel for online and mobile sales made to customers located in a particular store's catchment area. At these retailers, local sales teams do not view online sales as a lost commission opportunity, because they receive credit for all sales in their district, regardless of the channel.

Finally, HR processes will need to be adjusted. To build teams quickly, companies will have to hire tech-savvy managers externally as well as developing them internally. Their training should mix formal instruction with on-the-job learning. The latter might entail a buddy system that pairs new, digitally fluent employees with more experienced staff so that they learn from each other, mentorship programs for those in the organization who need to be brought up to speed in the new world, and rotation systems so that well-qualified young managers work closely with a range of senior managers in different parts of the business.

If the retailer is really low on digital know-how, a partnership, joint venture, or even acquisition might be required to bring in the necessary expertise. US department store Nordstrom went into partnership with the trendy men's clothing e-retailer Bonobos to tap its digital expertise, while Wal-Mart created @WalmartLabs through the purchase of Kosmix, a social-media start-up that builds and tests Web and mobile applications.

New organizational structures and governance

Adapting the organization to support the vision will entail rethinking organizational structures, as several of the more advanced retailers are already doing. Some are creating new, dedicated units. A leading consumer electronics chain has set up a cross-channel pricing unit to manage online and in-store prices, for example, because such highly specialized skills are required to manage pricing tools. Other retailers have created units devoted to engaging consumers through digital channels such as social media. Dedicated units might also be required to extract insights from big data; these would be staffed by people who combine analytical skills and an understanding of the business so that they know what to look for among the heaps of information. People who have both qualities are rare.

Other companies choose to improve coordination mechanisms. The proliferation of touch points and sales channels requires a high level of coordination among those channels and the functions that manage them. It is crucial that decisions on pricing or promotions are made with all channels in mind. The same applies to inventory management. It will therefore be important to assemble core teams to align decisions and mitigate potential channel conflict.

A change of governance structures will almost certainly be required. A formal governance structure of reporting lines and board and committee memberships signals to the organization that the technology strategy is a prime board concern, and it can help change attitudes. It is essential that, contrary to most current practice, the chief information officer (or chief technology officer) be a strong leader on the operating board or executive committee and that his or her role is seen as central to the board's decisions. Such structures can then be reinforced by other signals telling the organization that technology strategy is now at the heart of the organization. The CEO can stress the fact in internal and external communications, for example. Taking ownership of risky projects might mean more skin in the game, but that is why it has symbolic value. Similarly, finding ways to acknowledge and celebrate tech-related talent in the wider business is a powerful signal that, in cultural terms, technology matters.

A new managerial style also will be required. Agility in the digital era will demand a highly collaborative managerial approach—a major change in the traditional vertical command-and-control world of retail. Command chains should be short and flexible, so teams can be assembled and reassembled to take on different projects. Coordination and collaboration mechanisms must be strong to manage complexity and facilitate fast decision-making and innovation. Digital technologies not only permit but increasingly require managers and line staff to work in the shared virtual spaces of the intranet and cloud-hosted documents. Managers must learn to thrive in this environment, in the knowledge that the best decisions emerge from the input of many. And there must be willingness to learn from others. It would be eye opening for many senior retail executives to glimpse what is possible by visiting technological companies in South Korea or Silicon Valley, inviting "tech apostles" to executive meetings, and visiting start-ups.

Making it happen

So far, we have described three steps that many retailers must take to equip themselves for the future. They need to change their organization's mindset so that technology is integrated into everyone's thinking and actions. They need to set a new aspiration for the business, supported by a distinctive value proposition that will create long-term value. And they need to adapt the organization to make the aspiration a reality. We have also suggested ways in which some of this might be achieved. But it will be clear by now to any senior manager in a conventional, store-based retailer that what we are suggesting is a complete corporate transformation.

The transformation challenge

Unfortunately, research shows that more than 70 percent of companies that undertake change programs to achieve such transformations fail.[6] The reason? In large measure, behavior. More often than not, employees resist change, and managers who have typically been with the business for many years and have absorbed its old culture and ways of behaving do not support it either (Exhibit 7.1). Expecting organizations to transform themselves without an accompanying personal transformation of those it employs—starting with the CEO and other top managers—is unrealistic.

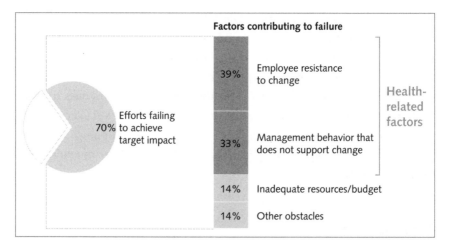

Exhibit 7.1 Barriers to organizational change.
Source: Scott Keller and Colin Price, *Beyond Performance: How Great Organizations Build Ultimate Competitive Advantage* (Hoboken, NJ: John Wiley & Sons, Inc., 2011), p. 23. This material is reproduced with permission of John Wiley & Sons, Inc.

Designing and driving change programs that address explicitly these behavioral (or "organizational health") issues is of paramount importance. McKinsey consultants Scott Keller and Colin Price have written about this in their book *Beyond Performance*, arguing that organizational health, as well as performance, needs to be addressed in each of five stages of a transformation.[7] In a 2010 survey of 2,512 executives at companies undergoing transformations,[8] companies that focused on the health of their organization as well as the traditional performance metrics were almost three times as successful as those that focused on performance only.[9]

Transformation principles

With this in mind, we consider six aspects of a transformation to be the most important ones for CEOs to contemplate when they embark on a technology-driven change program. We describe them here as six transformation principles.

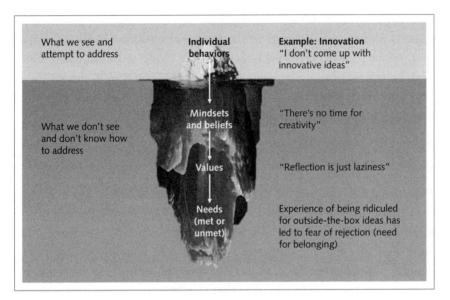

What we see and attempt to address	Individual behaviors	Example: Innovation "I don't come up with innovative ideas"
What we don't see and don't know how to address	Mindsets and beliefs	"There's no time for creativity"
	Values	"Reflection is just laziness"
	Needs (met or unmet)	Experience of being ridiculed for outside-the-box ideas has led to fear of rejection (need for belonging)

Exhibit 7.2 Drilling down to underlying mindsets.
Source: Scott Keller and Colin Price, *Beyond Performance: How Great Organizations Build Ultimate Competitive Advantage* (Hoboken, NJ: John Wiley & Sons, Inc., 2011), p. 94. This material is reproduced with permission of John Wiley & Sons, Inc.

1. Behavior changes only if mindsets change

A successful transformation eventually results in new behavior. But the beliefs and mindsets that control the behavior have to change first. For example, a retailer cannot run a successful bricks-and-clicks business if a store manager fails to help a customer looking for an out-of-stock item to find the item online and place the order in the store. Members of the sales staff need to see that the digital channel is a key element of the retailer's value proposition and the store managers should be the best role models.

Current beliefs and mindsets therefore need to be explored (Exhibit 7.2). For example, what are the beliefs that prevent someone from putting forward innovative ideas? Investigation may show that the person feels there is no time for creativity in the firm, that reflection is not valued, or that, given past experiences, new ideas are likely to be ridiculed. Once such beliefs and values are uncovered, steps can be taken to change them. This exploratory exercise should be conducted at a team and individual level, starting with the top managers.

2. Top team alignment powers the change

Behavioral change starts at the top. But if the behavior of top managers is to change, those managers must be aligned on the new aspiration and strategy, which in turn requires addressing the concerns and fears of the top team. Imagine, for example, a strategy that entails building a new, shared multichannel IT platform serving the entire global company. Country managers may well fear that this will compromise their ability to choose the types of solutions they need to run their local businesses successfully. Unless such concerns are addressed and the management team aligned, the country managers could slow down or even derail the transformation. And only with such alignment will the top team acquire the necessary shared sense of urgency and commitment to change, as well as a shared undertaking to make it happen, all of which will shape new behavior.

This stacking of hands will power the broader organizational shift, but it will require some honest conversations about reasons why the organization needs to change, individual concerns, and each person's role in the change. The scale of what is at stake more than justifies an investment of time by the board of directors or broader executive team in an intense period of education, reflection, and problem solving.

3. Use four levers to sustain new behavior

We have explained how transformations require behavioral change, which in turn requires new mindsets. But companies will need to use every means at their disposal to make the new behaviors take hold and really

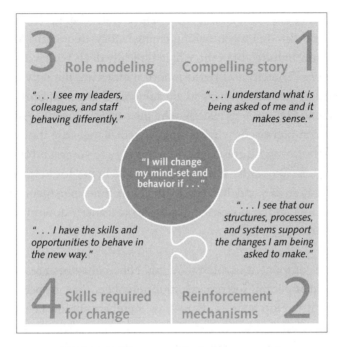

Exhibit 7.3 Elements of the influence model.
Source: Scott Keller and Colin Price, *Beyond Performance: How Great Organizations Build Ultimate Competitive Advantage* (Hoboken, NJ: John Wiley & Sons, Inc., 2011), p. 117. This material is reproduced with permission of John Wiley & Sons, Inc.

stick. The influence model can help. It has four components that reinforce each other when applied coherently (Exhibit 7.3).

The first component consists of the kind of organizational changes already discussed. The organization's day-to-day life must be seen to reflect the new ways of working and the planned changes. Employees need to see that structures and processes, such as cross-channel pricing, promotions, or performance management, are consistent with change and so support the new behaviors expected of them. These structures and processes are reinforcing mechanisms. Likewise, the organization's efforts to equip its employees with new skills and capabilities will convince employees that they *can* change their behavior and still work effectively in the new environment.

Two additional components will help ensure change is sustainable. One is the need to tell a compelling change story, frequently. Motivation resides mainly in the right brain, which typically deals with the big picture and emotions. Therefore, if performance metrics are the only objectives, radical change is unlikely. Instead, sustainable change requires a compelling story, one that explains exactly why the company needs to distinguish itself from competitors or why the envisioned changes are the only means of securing a strong future. And when it comes to successful transformations, the more frequently the story is told, the better for helping to align the organization beyond the top team. Each time managers repeat the story, they invoke the power of gravity to cascade it down through the organization.

The last component is role modeling. New behaviors are more likely to take hold if people see organization members they respect behaving differently. If the top team is aligned, its members should be natural role models (an effect that underlines the need for top management to be the first to start behaving differently). But senior role models cannot always just act in new ways and expect others to follow suit; they may have to ask others to change, and tell them when they fail to do so. Also, retailers embarking on a transformation should identify additional educators and evangelists to help win over the skeptics. Organizations should even consider putting them in charge of some of the most important initiatives.

4. Perseverance, rigor, and flexibility are required

Transformation journeys are long and hard, making them feel like a daily 20-mile march. Frequently, particularly after the launch of pilot projects, the skeptics will make their feelings heard, and local loyalties will surface. At such times, perseverance and rigor will be required to make sure lessons learned are captured. But as companies experiment and grow wiser, they will inevitably have to adapt the original road map, requiring that rigor be overlaid with flexibility—a difficult balance. Do not expect to have all the answers on day one of the journey.

5. Mix projects that have short- and medium-term impact

To keep people on board during the transformation, it is important to have a mix of initiatives with short- and medium-term impact. These might combine pilots for learning and engaging the organization, some quick-win projects that offer a glimpse of what the future might hold, and a few large-scale initiatives that will take longer to show results. Impact is the only fuel for change, and companies need to plan so that successes are evident. For the same reason, the projects should engage as many people in the organization as possible. Research shows that change programs designed and implemented in a way that ensures extensive collaboration across the organization are 1.5 times more likely to succeed than those not promoting collaboration.[10]

6. Success is equated with CEO involvement

Perhaps the most important lesson is the amount of leadership that a successful transformation requires from the CEO. Delegation is not an option. Our CEO survey shows that transformations with strong CEO leadership and heavy CEO involvement at all levels are more than twice as likely to be successful as those with uninvolved leaders.[11] There is no single recipe for successful senior-leadership involvement, since the nature of the role will be influenced by many characteristics, such as scale of the transformation and the leader's personal style. Nevertheless, strong leadership includes four key roles: making the transformation meaningful by telling an impactful change story, modeling new behaviors and encouraging people, building a strong leadership team, and getting personally involved (e.g. by making critical decisions quickly and making the team accountable).

* * *

The changes the retail industry is undergoing are no less profound than those brought about by the mercantile revolution in the Middle Ages, when an embryonic banking system made capital funding available for the first time, and the Industrial Revolution at the turn of the 21st century, which ushered in mass production and the consumer society. Retailing now finds itself in the grips of a digital revolution. There is little doubt that, as with any revolution, not all will survive. Those that do will need a crystal-clear understanding of the challenges they face. And many retailers that began life operating stores will need to change the way they think about their businesses to accommodate the fact that technology is driving this revolution and that technology will touch almost every aspect of the old business model. Once retailers have accepted this new reality, they will need to set an entirely new aspiration for their companies, then muster all their resources and embark upon a corporate transformation that will make that aspiration a reality.

CEOs may understandably feel daunted by what they are required to take on. Never have retailers been asked to cope with so much change, so fast. Given the amount of involvement that will be required over an extended period to make the transformation, some CEOs may conclude that the challenge is best left to the next management team. But there is another way of looking at today's retailing environment. These developments are of an epochal nature. Thus, the chance to play a part in them is a privilege, and companies cannot fail to learn in the process. Moreover, retail managers who engage with the opportunities, get out of the office, see other stores, meet technologists, and talk to partners in the value chain about what the future holds will, in all likelihood, find themselves imbued with an irresistible sense of excitement and conviction that they must act.

Notes

1. McKinsey iConsumer research, 2011 and 2010.
2. Nielsen Co., *State of the Nation 2012: A Review of UK Consumers and the Grocery Industry in 2011*, p. 151; Nielsen Co., *State of the Nation 2008: Online Shopping*, p. 6.
3. Eurostat, "Internet purchases by individuals," http://appsso.eurostat.ec. europa.eu/nui/show.do?dataset=isoc_ec_ibuy&lang=en.

4. United Nations. Department of Economic and Social Affairs, Population database available at http://esa.un.org/unpd/wpp/Excel-Data/population.htm, accessed January 23, 2013. Data for Western Europe include France, Germany, Italy, the Netherlands, Norway, Spain, Sweden, and the United Kingdom.

5. "In business NRF 2011: Multichannel comes of age," *Retail Week*, January 21, 2011.

6. Scott Keller and Colin Price, *Beyond Performance: How Great Organizations Build Ultimate Competitive Advantage* (Hoboken, NJ: John Wiley & Sons, Inc., 2011).

7. Scott Keller and Colin Price, *Beyond Performance: How Great Organizations Build Ultimate Competitive Advantage* (Hoboken, NJ: John Wiley & Sons, Inc., 2011), pp. 18–20.

8. Scott Keller *et al.*, "What successful transformations share," *McKinsey Quarterly*, March 2010.

9. Overall success was self-evaluated by executives in a survey on a four-point rating scale: extremely successful, very successful, somewhat successful, and not at all successful.

10. Scott Keller and Colin Price, *Beyond Performance: How Great Organizations Build Ultimate Competitive Advantage* (Hoboken, NJ: John Wiley & Sons, Inc., 2011), p. 72. Overall success has been self-evaluated by executives in a survey on a four-point rating scale: extremely successful, very successful, somewhat successful, and not at all successful.

11. Scott Keller and Colin Price, *Beyond Performance: How Great Organizations Build Ultimate Competitive Advantage* (Hoboken, NJ: John Wiley & Sons, Inc., 2011), p. 203–206.

ACKNOWLEDGMENTS

Writing this book has been a rewarding journey. Rewarding, because we were spending time on a topic that really excites us. Rewarding, because we had such illuminating conversations with industry leaders and experts across the globe. And rewarding, because we had the pleasure of working with a great team of McKinsey colleagues.

Among the many people from the industry with whom we talked, we would like to thank in particular (and in alphabetical order) Massimo Bongiovanni, Stéphane Bout, Peter Fitzgerald, Federico Marchetti, Dev Mukherjee, Steve Nigro, Diego Piacentini, David Porter, and Hervé Thoumyre. They sat down with us for intensive discussions, offered some stunning insights and opinions about where the industry is heading and acted as engaged thought partners. While all responsibility for the views in this book lies with the authors, those views would have been greatly diminished without their participation. Within McKinsey, we had many, many valuable discussions and we would like to thank in particular Andres Hoyos-Gomez, Dilip Wagle and Karel Dörner.

Once we had a first draft of the book, we asked a sounding board of senior retailer experts to review it and we would like to thank our colleagues Klaus Behrenbeck, Jesko Perrey, and Dennis Spillecke, as well as Christoph Lütke Schelhowe and Massimo Bongiovanni, for their constructive and encouraging feedback.

This book is the result of a team effort. Foremost, we would like to thank our co-authors for their enormous contributions and enthusiasm: Nina Gillmann, James Naylor, Roger Roberts, and Lis Strenger. Important parts of the research were done by Sabine Bechtle, Britta Lietke, Bary Pradelski, Ewa Sikora, Patrick Simon, and Fabian Struckand. Gabriella Picca and Lena Rembold have been integral members of the team throughout our journey, and Karen Schenkenfelder helped us tremendously with proofreading and copy-editing. We are truly grateful for all the time and effort each of our colleagues put in to make this happen.

And finally, we would like to thank Joanne Mason for her guidance, patience, and absolutely crucial editing work.

ABOUT THE AUTHORS

Stefan Niemeier is a Director of McKinsey & Company and leads its European "Technology in Retail" group. He has advised retailers around the globe and across many retail sub-sectors. Stefan holds a PhD in Economics and a Masters in Business Administration.

Andrea Zocchi is a Director of McKinsey & Company where he leads the Consumer Practice in Southern Europe. Andrea is also an adjunct professor at IMT—Institute for Advanced Studies—in Lucca (Italy), where he teaches a PhD level course on advanced problem-solving techniques. Andrea holds a degree in Mechanical Engineering and prior to joining McKinsey, he worked for Hewlett Packard Italy.

Marco Catena is an Associate Principal of McKinsey & Company. He works with retail and mobile telecommunications players in Europe on commercial and performance transformation topics. Marco holds a PhD in Industrial Management and a Degree in Management Engineering.

James Naylor is a Senior Knowledge Expert in McKinsey & Company's European Retail Practice, concentrating on latest and best practice in retail format development and on the development of consumer goods industries in emerging markets. James holds Undergraduate and Masters degrees in Psychology.

Roger Roberts is an Expert Partner in the Silicon Valley office of McKinsey & Company and leads the firm's IT service lines for North American Consumer Goods and Retail businesses. He also serves a range of clients across sectors on adapting to technology-based disruptions. Roger holds engineering degrees from Stanford University and an MBA from MIT's Sloan School of Management where he has served on the board of the MIT Center for Digital Business.

Nina Gillmann is a Consultant of McKinsey & Company. Nina has advised some of the world's largest corporations on strategic and operational issues, with an industry focus in retail and advanced industries. She holds a Diploma in Economics from the University of Kiel as well as a Master of Letters from the University of St Andrews and a PhD in Political Sciences from the University of Kiel.

Lis Hannemann-Strenger is a Consultant of McKinsey & Company. She works in the Consumer Practice on strategy and transformation topics. Lis holds a PhD and Masters in Business Administration.

INDEX

Compiled by Indexing Specialists (UK) Ltd., Indexing House, 306A Portland Road, Hove, East Sussex BN3 5LP United Kingdom.